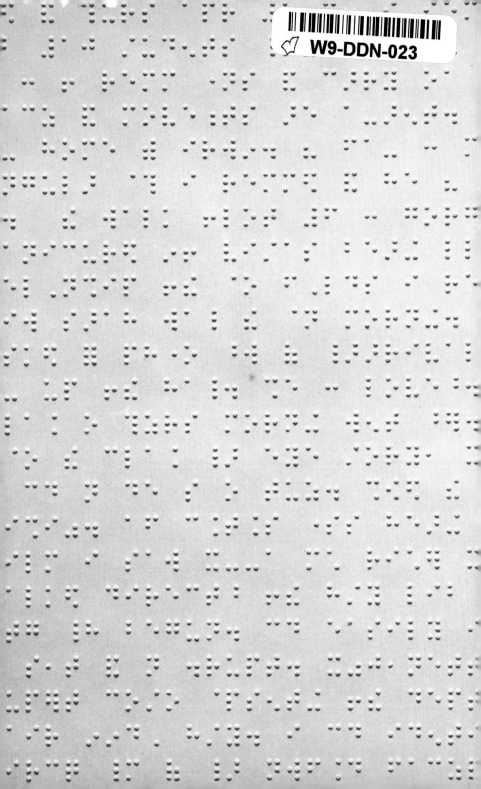

SECOND SIGHT

Robert V. Hine

SECOND SIGHT

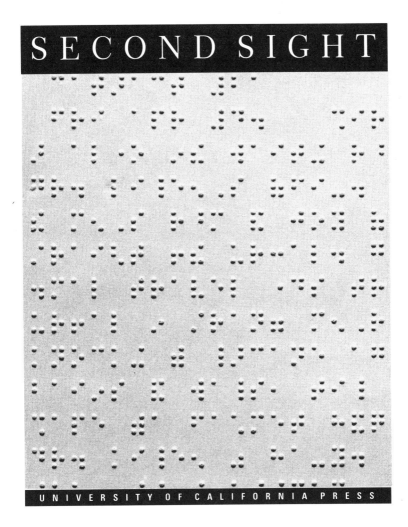

UNIVERSITY OF CALIFORNIA PRESS

Berkeley Los Angeles London

The publisher wishes to thank Delacorte Press
for permission to print an excerpt from their book
Selected Poems, 1923–1967 by Jorge Luis Borges.

University of California Press
Berkeley and Los Angeles, California

University of California Press
London, England

Library of Congress Cataloging-in-Publication Data
Hine, Robert V., 1921–
    Second sight / by Robert V. Hine.
        p.   cm.
    Includes bibliographical references and index.
    ISBN 0-520-08195-1 (alk. paper)
    1. Hine, Robert V., 1921—Health.   2. Blind—United States—
Biography.   I. Title.
RE36.H56A3   1993
362.4′1′092—dc20
[B]
                                            92-31096
                                               CIP

Printed in the United States of America

2   3   4   5   6   7   8   9

The paper used in this publication meets the minimum
requirements of American National Standard for Information
Sciences—Permanence of Paper for Printed Library Materials,
ANSI Z39.48-1984 ♾

The title page and endsheets show extracts from the author's
braille journal, kept during the restoration of his sight. The language is grade-three braille, a shorthand version of standard grade
two. The passage on the title page is for Friday, April 4 (found on
page 137); the passages on the book's endsheets are for Good
Friday, March 28 (left-hand endsheet; passage found on page 114),
and for Wednesday and Thursday, April 2–3 (right-hand endsheet;
passage found on page 131). The contents and illustrations pages
display the braille alphabet, while each chapter opening page includes a braille transcription of the chapter title.

For all my family

And for the woman who in one half hour
brought them back to me,
Jeanne L. Killeen, M.D.

Contents

Illustrations

(Illustrations appear on overleaf)

1. Robert and Shirley Hine, 1987
(During the year following surgery)

2. Author in office about 1983
(Note braille labels on books)
(Courtesy Riverside *Press-Enterprise*, Greg Crowder)

3. Author in office about 1985
(Note talking computer)
(Courtesy Riverside *Press-Enterprise*, Dave Bauman)

2

3

Preface

Transitions may be traumatic and instructive, especially when they stand between sight and blindness or between blindness and sight. When I realized that I would see again after fifteen years of blindness, the trauma seemed instructive enough to begin a detailed journal of my reactions, first in braille, and then, as the pages became clearer and clearer, by hand. Later when eyes grown sluggish accustomed themselves reluctantly and gradually to the printed page, I began reading books by blind people. There was some compulsion. It was not just the excitement of regained sight. I needed to understand what had happened to me, the lost and the regained. Perhaps the experiences of others could tell me what was going on inside myself. But it was not Homer, Samson, Helen Keller, or John Milton who helped me most; rather, it was the moderns who cope with a complex, sordid world.

In John Hull, for example, I found a fellow professor who

plumbed the meaning of his experience like an oracle. For him blindness is "whole-body-seeing," substituting the total body for one organ. It is a "terrible gift." Hull is not an Isaiah making darkness into light; instead, he "considers how his light is spent" as if he were in *Paradise Lost* seeking God in the dark realms of the fallen angels.

I found a blind mystical Frenchman, Jacques Lusseyran, who speaks from the French Resistance and from the horrors of Buchenwald. Blindness for him is not darkness, which comes only when he is afraid or angry or ill. He lives in a world flooded by light: "At every waking hour and even in my dreams I lived in a stream of light." "I was the prisoner of light. I was condemned to see."

I found Eleanor Clark, a highly literate, richly poetic, and elegantly witty writer, tennis player and skier, Connecticut mother of two, novelist, recipient of a National Book Award, and full participant in the cultural world of her husband, Robert Penn Warren. She finds little in blindness to like: "Who says you have to accept it, experience it, still less relish it?" Her conclusion: "by hook, crook or Trojan horse, to work."

People like Hull and Lusseyran are indeed heroic, because they have gone beyond courage to find a new world. They are the shout on the other side of silence. But I must confess to many a day when I could identify only with Clark, alternately yelling and grumping.

Sometimes I think Hull and Lusseyran do not represent blindness but only theology or mysticism. And I am neither theologian nor mystic, just a university professor writing books about the wild and woolly American West. How much do I share with them? Is Clark my real spokesperson? I wonder how the ideas of any of them would change were they granted the miracle of second sight.

In the end I was engaging in a discourse between two kinds of experience. Karl Bjarnhof tells of a Danish boy who gouged his sightless eyes until they hurt so he could see shooting stars. Blind, bloody shooting stars were not those of the astronomer, yet the boy's were every bit as verifiable, as authentic. I can only faintly imagine what it was like for the blind Ved Mehta to pedal his bicycle through the campus at Claremont. There are different kinds of transition, too. Andrew Potok forcefully argues that writer-historians have no blind problems compared with him, a painter. Sally Wagner might laughingly utter "Balderdash" from her Kansas City news desk. I heard Robert Murphy and Tom Sullivan counter that the really active man, the athlete, was the most pathetic disabled figure. James Thurber only smiled, told a family story, and as his sight faded, drew his dogs with simpler and simpler lines.

It was not that I argued with them. I came to love them, like a rambunctious family that apparently could not agree on much but actually agreed on a great deal. I knew blindness for a longer period than Hull or Clark, for a shorter period than many of the others, but I also knew the restoration of sight. If I bring to my encounter even a measure of the perceptivity of these other members of the family, I ask for no more.

SECOND SIGHT

Leadville

At the age of twenty, who believes a crotchety old doctor telling him that he would be blind? The man sat there with his round-mirrored reflector tilted on his forehead like a cartoon Cyclops and intoned that my blindness would come eventually, probably sooner than later, and I should start preparing—learn braille, arrange for mobility training, all those jolly pastimes for a recent teenager. The place was a doctor's cold office in Denver, where I had not been before and have never been since (either the doctor's office or the city). I don't think I said much. Being dutiful, I thanked him, I guess. I had seen a lot of doctors, but none had ever told me that.

The bus ride back into the frozen Rockies, to Leadville where I was then living, alone, was dreary enough, bleak March in Colorado, but, strangely, I don't remember it as anything like a scene from *Wuthering Heights*—no depressing journey, no long last look at sun and snow and human faces, no tearful tirade against fate. Where were the violins? Twenty-year-olds do not rail and shake their fists at fortune. Statistics do not include them. Predictions are for others. Cart away the Delphic priestess and all her medical counterparts to a retirement home where they belong.

Or was it my temperament, not my age? Dutiful, yes. That makes me an ordinary sort of person, not given to railing. In the first place, it would embarrass me to wail about blindness, and I do not like to be embarrassed. When I think back over the silly things, far less traumatic events, that have caused me mortification! I still feel the chagrin of a night in a crowded car of teenagers when Sylvia rode on my lap. She had sort of snuggled up, and I felt stirrings within me, but it was the conversation that followed. Heartlessly, in a loud voice, she asked what I had in my pocket. Without thinking, I blurted out, "A flashlight." Funny thing is that it was true. I did have a small pocket flashlight there, but what cost, truth. I just wanted to be anywhere else.

Even as a grown man I blush when the conversation

gets beyond me. I worry about elemental discussions of sex and money. I broke up with Sylvia but not before she told me I needed green socks; I was just too gray and brown.

So it was a gray and brown me who rode that lonely bus back to Leadville. And I endured the first open news of blindness with a shrug. I was not that badly off. It was hard to feel sorry for myself. Not that I couldn't have. My eyes were only the tip of an iceberg. What I had really been fighting for years was a damnable case of juvenile rheumatoid arthritis. Not too long after Sylvia, huge bulbar, inflamed knees and elbows and wrists, in fact every joint, including my jaws, had stiffened and pained, and that lasted for years. I consumed salicylates like popcorn. I spent my seventeenth year immobilized in bed. The joints grew so locked that they had to be literally broken loose by husky therapists in a warm-water swimming pool. Even so, my knees and elbows remained so deformed that they would neither straighten nor contract beyond fifteen or twenty degrees. I could never again assume the fetal position and so was at least insured against certain forms of insanity.

But so what? That was largely in the past, and who feels sorry for the past? Now on that stinking bus from

Denver we curved slowly back to the slushy streets of Leadville. The bus was full, for it was World War II, and Leadville was booming, bustling to produce lead and copper and molybdenum for the guns of the Allies. I slouched back to meals at Mrs. Powell's boarding-house with fifteen men around a threadbare oilcloth table. I only knew the others' first names—Louie, Rivers, Swisher, Dum-dum. Once boxers, longshoremen, lumberjacks, whistlepunks, now they were double-jack drivers or mill hands, released from the army or deferred by their draft boards to man the vital mines. They were happy to be out of uniform but not to be there; "Goddamned slaves," they called themselves. That horny-handed bunch never knew what to make of me, a stumbling college kid in dark glasses who worked peeling brussels sprouts.

Louie Blaine from Montrose was the only one I could really appeal to. He seemed to like me. He took me up to his bunk room once to give me some ore samples ("swell rock chunks from the Leadville mines," I called them in my journal). The attic room was filled with beds at all angles and clothes hanging from slant-ing rafters. On one bed sat a miner playing long mournful notes on a bugle. Somehow I could tell Louie about my eyes. He didn't say much, but the image of that room remains strong—lonely men, and that included me, yearning for women and home, trapped in places they didn't want to be, Sartre's existential characters looking for an exit that wasn't there.

Louie took me to his workplace once, too, where he mucked at the Resurrection up in California Gulch. He showed me the great crushers smashing four-foot chunks of ore into powder, the flotation vats with suds boiling up the minerals. They seemed to give him joy and a reason for being. I wished I had something like that. Louie was a good friend. He seemed to understand my predicament. We sometimes drank coffee quietly at Murphy's Bar.

I roomed on Harrison Street, upstairs in the Victorian gingerbread house of Mrs. Strong. The town was so bursting that I had not been able to find room and board in one place, so I ate at Mrs. Powell's and slept about two blocks away at Mrs. Strong's. My quarters were hardly bigger than the single bed, but I had a small table in front of a window that looked out over dreary mud and snow to the post office and across Harrison Street to the square spire of the Presbyterian church. Friends had given me an electric record player and a few records. I alternated mindlessly and ad infinitum between a Bach Brandenburg concerto and

Debussy's "Nuages" while I wrote long letters home on stormy Sunday afternoons.

Since my eyes were continually dilated, I wore dark glasses, always outside and sometimes in brightly lighted rooms. As I hunched along Leadville streets in a heavy coat and smoked lenses, I knew that the dogs did not like me. I wrote home:

> There are more dogs per square inch in Leadville than any other part of the country, I'm sure. They roam all over the place, alone and in groups of five or six, and they range in size from Chihuahuas to St. Bernards. When I was a newcomer with my alpaca coat and dark glasses, I was an object of persecution by these numerous hounds, and they would all bark at me and some would growl at my feet as I walked along the street. All the old-timers have scars where they have been bitten by dogs. As soon as a dog bites a couple of people in a row, the police just come along and shoot him. Now, however, as my coat and glasses have become known throughout the dog world as not belonging to a Martian invasion or a bandit from the 1890s, the dogs have accepted me and no longer bark. Instead they jump and run along beside me in

play and fun. So one aspect of Leadville is
conquered.

That ending was obviously for a mother's consumption. I don't remember that the dogs ever did anything but bark and snarl.

The reason I was in Leadville was itself rather curious. The arthritis left me with an eye condition known as uveitis, more specifically, iridocyclitis. For both diseases, the doctors tried everything—concocting over time a witch's stew of salicylates, calcium glutomate, intravenous gold injections, intramuscular foreign protein (Proteolac), bee stings by mouth, intravenous typhoid fever inducement (literally!), intramuscular liver extract (that was a surprisingly painful one), tuberculosis skin injections, intramuscular penicillin, brucella vaccine. I suspected a note of desperation when my California doctor, John Lordan, suggested living at least six months in a high altitude. Elevation, he explained, increases white blood count, and those increased antibodies would marshal their battalions against the arthritis and the uveitis.

It was early in World War II. Movement was not that easy. My father was working in a shipyard. My mother was involved with the two other kids. A great aunt would come over and say, "You mean you're going to send that poor crippled boy to live alone somewhere, just because a doctor thinks something might happen with white corpuscles? He's only guessing. What does he know?"

What did anybody know? But that was like my family: everyone had to have his or her say. The expense would be a problem for my father, but I figured I could get a job and pay for some of it. Besides, it seemed a whole lot more fun than the typhoid injections. Except for my brother and sister, the family generally took their protective-buffer stance. They had seen me through the years of rheumatoid arthritis and had no desire to see me regress. But they had to admit that now I was able to get around pretty well, and in the end, what else was there to do? We had tried most everything, and there was an elementary logic to this idea. All it took was a little money for the train and a bit more to support me until I could get a job.

My mother was a reader. At nineteen she had tasted the intellectual life at Berkeley and dreamed of writing for a newspaper before she eloped with my twenty-year-old father and gave birth to me. Now she reluctantly pulled out her gazetteer, placed it on the kitchen table, and searched for the highest town of any consequence in the continental United States. It turned out to be Leadville, Colorado, 10,200 feet above sea level, plenty high to change blood count. So Leadville would supply the altitude; my parents, the train ticket. The leukocytes would do the rest.

The Denver and Rio Grande let me off on a freezing day in January at an improbable Leadville station in a godforsaken sweep about two or three miles into nowhere. A ramshackle bus took me to the town. When I got my room and board settled, I walked down Harrison Street in the crunching snow and saw a Help Wanted sign in the Safeway store. I got the job then and there, tending the produce. That smug companion, Independence, walked back with me to my room, where I wrote home.

A couple of weeks later I came to my room and found a telegram from my mother and father. Stop working at the Safeway immediately, the square letters spelled out, and they implied that my doctor felt that such work, lifting vegetable boxes, might endanger the cure. I can imagine the arguments that had gone on at home after they heard that I was working in a grocery store: he's lifting those heavy crates, straining the delicate veins in his eyes. We must check with the doctor.

It was hard for me to swallow the disappointment. My letter home the next day tried to be positive.

Last night your telegram arrived, and I still do not understand. I showed the telegram to Steve this morning (he's the manager of the store) and he said of course you mustn't work if it's going to do any harm and was very nice about it. Since all the days I've worked I have been learning the job, I didn't want him to pay me for them, but he insisted on doing so. I am anxious to get your letter to know the reasons, for it seemed to me that everything was working perfectly.

I do not still have their letter of explanation, which came a few days later. But my response to that letter concealed the gamut of emotions.

I was disappointed to find in your letter that there were no doctor's orders to quit the job. I really do not think it would have hurt me, but if it makes you happier why I of course will not work. Maybe later on I can find a job which would suit better.

So back I went to the lonely streets with the dogs and my dark glasses, sleeping twelve hours at night and three hours in the day. That was clearly a measure of boredom. It's a wonder I did not turn to crime, or at least vice! But I labored under the illusion that so much sleep would aid the cure.

As I walked up and down to my room, just to the right of the coiled banister and creaking stairway, I passed a dark room with yellowing eye charts and dusty scopes, the former office of Dr. J. C. Strong, an ophthalmologist. Now his widow fearfully took in us roomers upstairs, but she had not disturbed her husband's space. That unused office was an eerie augury, portent of a long line of cheerless ophthalmologists' offices awaiting me.

You may have already guessed. The leukocytes of Leadville, lazy critters, did not work. Many times during that frigid time I hoped and thought that they were doing their job. When there were temporary thaws in the weather (so temporary in Leadville winters), I was sure that the precipitates in my eyes were melting, too. On January 30, for example, I wrote in my journal,

I can say truthfully that my right eye has noticeably improved vision. Outlines are still very fuzzy, but objects can be distinguished with a fair amount of ease.

In March, however, the old fiery redness and sandy discomfort, telltale signs of a uveitis flare-up, led me to board the bus down the Continental Divide for a medical look-see in Denver. That's where I got the black news. Neither the snow nor the precipitate had really gone, and as I look back now through that journal, I was not only being unduly optimistic but also unconsciously noting sounds more often than sights. For example, aware like a Californian of such things, I described the winter: "New snow rustles as the wind blows it across the old snow." "New snow is soft and silent as you walk on it." "Old snow crunches." I was beginning my long descent into Arctic twilight. Primary senses were changing.

On the bus ride back from Denver, maybe I reacted so little because a part of me knew it would happen. I may well have been resigned to becoming blind, though it was twenty years before the fact. Yet since the sprigs of hope are symbiotic, smothering like dodder the vines of acceptance, it is hard to know when realization finally comes. And I still do not know when individual members of my family came to understand that I would be blind.

Did my father realize it? I wonder. He was too much the optimist, a superstitious gambler at heart, and gambling is one way to deny reality. He gambled on the Bible and once read it through, doggedly, word by word every night in bed before it fell from his hands in sleep, without understanding, without joy, because the act was itself a protective talisman from the world around him. He spit in his itchy palm and rubbed it in his pocket because that brought money. So too did the bubbles on coffee, each one worth a dollar if you got them into your mouth before they broke. He would drive miles out of his way to avoid a black cat crossing the street. To him, these were not idle jokes. And deep down he must have felt that my blindness could be conquered by his legions of good luck. Still there were weekends when he would disappear, taking off for Tijuana.

My mother was more rational, but she was far more emotional and sentimental. She could cry at the mere mention of a suffering animal. Accepting my illness must have been hard for her, and she probably never faced the likelihood of my blindness, perhaps until she died, for she succumbed to cancer in 1963 before my vision had dropped terribly low.

My brother and sister are twins, eight years my junior. They were just starting their teens when I went to Leadville. Dick was a free spirit, always active, but with some of our mother's sentiment. I remember him as a boy crying over a dismembered dying insect. Patty appreciated school far less than she enjoyed the boys, and she was liked by everyone. It seemed to me that Patty and Dick coped pretty well. Suddenly their only older brother ceased to provide any kind of physical role model, became a constant drain on their parents' attention, and required explanation to their friends. But that was primarily because of the arthritic deformities. I always thought that for them my blindness was remote, unthinkable. Now I learn that for my sister, at least, through all those years my sight was her wish on every star and every birthday candle.

My mother's sister, our Aunt Katherine, known to everyone as Aunty, lived with us, too. She was particularly close to us kids, having practically raised my brother and sister. When arthritis immobilized me, she set up her own combat battalion. She rubbed my knees and elbows with liniments. She boiled whole grapefruit for hours and fed me the extract. She administered the bee stings. She heated oil in big cans and immersed my joints in them. And when the eyes became involved, she insisted on hot compresses. Given her dogged determination, I cannot believe she ever supposed my blindness was anything but reversible.

My acceptance, whenever it came, was quiet. So, if someone thinks of himself as a pacifist, how far does he go in carrying on a fight? An awful array of treatments had already proved unavailing. At what point would Mahatma Gandhi or Henry David Thoreau or Thomas Merton simply accept? Weren't there other matters on the agenda, like, for me, writing poetry about blood on the moon, drafting peace treaties, and planning leagues of nations?

Maybe there is something wrong with not fighting back. Why do I admire feisty Eleanor Clark, the writer who went blind? She alternated between fury ("Go away, get under there with the snakes. I'm sick of you") and anguish ("Secretly I yell No, no! and shut my ears, or they shut themselves"). Give me, she said, "a good, healthy capacity for gloom and despair."

That I avoided such gloom and despair I say with no bravado. It makes me feel even more an unheroic, ordinary person in need of green socks. Certainly I felt that way in Leadville—draft age, not even working for my keep, a traveler on trains filled with men in uniform.

The joints began to bother me. The white blood count was not working. It seemed time to scuttle Leadville and get on with things. My sight remained adequate, and however subconsciously, I slowly let the Denver curse grow dormant and tucked it away with the memories of Louie and his cohorts at Mrs. Powell's. With what vision and mobility I had, I went back to college, graduated in history, and was elected to Phi Beta Kappa.

Most important of all, I married Shirley, a wonderful woman who never told me to wear green socks; she took me as I was. When we were married, my vision was 20/100 in the good eye, 20/200 in the weaker left one, corrected to 20/50 and 20/100. That was plenty strong to see Shirley's long, straight, blond hair curled in around her neck. It belied her strength and hardiness. She made me promise never to say that I was doing something for her own good. Her intense blue eyes told me she would persist, and, though she knew the risks of marrying a man with my joints and eyes, I think she saw a kindred quality of persistence in me.

We took those risks together, and they outdid any gamble of working at the Leadville Safeway. The first big one was graduate school, all the way to Yale. New Haven winters were as rough as Leadville, and graduate study in history is for the best of retinas an invitation to problems; for one who had been consigned to braille, it verged on madness. But Shirley expressed no doubts. She took a job as the first woman receptionist at the Winchester Repeating Arms factory.

(She later happened to see her interview form; it had "Blond +" penciled on the top.) We lived in the rented upstairs room of a Polish Jewish widow who subsisted on the white meat of chicken boiled with carrots the size of untended zucchini. She gave the broth to us, gallons of it. We persisted rather well, and you might chalk up the staving off of trouble to those gallons of broth.

The Ph.D. brought us back to California, first to a fellowship at the Huntington Library in San Marino and then to teaching in the liberal arts college newly opened on the Riverside campus of the University of California. That was 1954, some dozen years after my sentence of blindness. Things were going well. I let the grim decree of Denver be swallowed up by rationalizations on the fallibility of doctors. The eyes still harbored their uveitis, but that was a nuisance I could live with. I sat for interminable hours in medical waiting rooms, none as dusty and dark as Dr. Strong's in Leadville, and I must admit that, in spite of light carpets and decorator prints, the visits had a way of calling up the old interior anguish. During those years I put in eyedrops morning and night—atropine, duboisine, scopolamine, or neosynephrine—to keep the iris open so the precipitates within would not stick it forever shut.

When cortisone became the wonder drug, I daily squeezed in Neo-DeltaCortef or dropped in Aristocort to calm the inflammation. There were other drops and salves through the years. Still, all these appointments and medications grew routine. I never mentioned them to outsiders, even people who knew me well at the university; I would as soon have told them I brushed my teeth.

My doctor for the majority of those years was Emma Mueller, a stern, no-nonsense German ophthalmologist at Kaiser Permanente in Fontana. I saw her every few months. After a long wait and a vision test, I would typically be seated in a chair that combined the graces of an old-fashioned dentist's and an electric executioner's. I knew just where and when to jut my chin in the brace of the slit lamp. Dr. Mueller clicked that blinding beam so it shone brighter and brighter as she drew it like a klieg light across the night-interior of the eyeball. When I first saw her, she took the pressure, like all doctors before her, by placing two fingertips on the top of the eyeball and alternately pressing like a hunt-and-peck typist to judge the pressure. But soon technological advances caused her to stretch me out on a table, place a drop mechanically in each eye (an anesthetic, I think), and position on my eyeball an early version of the tonometer. It was like a tiny scale of justice on which a little arm swung up and gave her a pressure reading.

Then she would write a few lines in my chart and swing around to say, "Mr. Hine, I find little change. Continue the drops as before and see me in three months."

In the late 1950s, she explained that cataracts were developing; no one could say how fast they might grow; she would keep an eye on them. The cortisone was very likely causing the cataracts, but since the cortisone was thought to be and probably was keeping the uveitis at bay, and since uveitis could itself cause cataracts, treatment went on as before. In 1967 I finished five years as chairman of the history department. Between then and 1970 the cataracts grew like hotbeds of spurge on a humid summer day.

Vision dramatically clouded. These were what Albert Vajda, who in London walked a similar path to blindness, called "the Gauze Ages." During that time layers of haze and floaters, swirls of lazily moving clots, became frenzied when I moved from bright light to darkness.

I went through scores of magnifying systems, hand-held glasses, round and square, tiny telescopes, devices that rested on the page, lenses suspended on frames with light beneath. "Great fish eyes leering up from beside bed or telephone," Clark called them, and "baby googlies crawling around bureau drawers."

"The next time I hear the word 'aids' I intend to misbehave." Those were her words, not mine.

I began writing with felt pens, and the letters got larger and larger. Notes for my lectures were in black blocked words, eventually so large that a page would take six lines from top to bottom. And the gauze between got thicker and thicker.

But, you ask, if I was going blind from cataracts, why not surgically remove them? The cataract operation alone would not have been that big a deal. It was the uveitis that caused the hitch. That delicate condition would not take kindly to the disturbance of surgery. Certain and total blindness, I was often told, was a likely possibility. I asked the question, however, times without count. In the end the dutiful temperament won out, for at heart I trusted the doctors.

Dr. Mueller was good in seeking other opinions. She called in three fellow ophthalmologists of Kaiser Permanente (Drs. Winters, Aiken, and Ousmanski). Some of them felt that surgery for removal of the cataracts was something to consider since there was so little to be lost, especially in the left eye, which had already grown far worse than the right. They admitted there was real danger, including a flare-up in the right eye, sympathetic opthalmia, as a result of surgery on the left. And beyond blindness there was always the possibility of disfigurement along with far more intense pain. I took that as a particular trauma—pain covering up how repulsive your eyes might look to others.

We went outside of Kaiser, too, to Dr. Ray Irvine in a Wilshire Boulevard overstuffed suite. He pressed his fingers on the eyeball so hard that I saw red, and indeed he asked me what color I saw. In the good eye, I recognized red; in the poor one, nothing. The good eye, he wrote, "had lardaceous keratic precipitates with central corneal edema and a white immature cortical cataract. There was early band keratopathy [deposits of calcium in one layer of the cornea] noted at the limbus [the margin of the cornea nearest the sclera]." The same was true in the bad eye, but in it the "anterior cornea was opaque and the cataract was mature." The intraocular pressure was soft in both eyes, especially the bad one. His conclusion regarding removal of the cataracts: Don't touch the left one; there isn't a ghost of a chance there. On the right eye,

I would be very hesitant to operate. . . . It has been my experience that cataracts in active rheumatoid arthritis do not respond well to surgery, and one has a great chance of enhancing the inflammatory process and causing the eye to go under atrophy such as has happened in the left eye.

He talked with Dr. Vernon Wong who worked with ophthalmic problems in arthritics at the National Institutes of Health in Washington, D.C. Wong was noncommittal. Dr. Samuel J. Kimura, a researcher at the University of California Medical Center in San Francisco with experience in this kind of problem, advised Irvine on the diagnosis but would not venture a conclusion on surgery. There was clearly no stirring battle cry for surgery; indeed, the voices of caution seemed more convincing to me, and I stayed, wearing my brown and gray socks, until the vision was gone.

By 1970, when I was forty-nine, the right eye with the strongest and best correction was 20/800; the left eye could discern only hand movements at three feet. Within a year or two neither eye had more than vague light perception. If the sun were coming through a window, I knew the difference between that and a blank wall. Like Dante, "In the middle of the journey of our life I came to myself in a dark wood where the straight way was lost." From there on, as far as I could tell, it was white canes and braille all the way. "Nyah, nyah, nyah," said Denver, "I told you so."

Metamorphosis

The gradual descent into the gray world was hardly like Dante's dreadful journey. My effort was more like spreading tendrils of adaptation working their way through new earth. Experimentation was called for. A good lecture in history, for example, involves reading and quoting, not only from letters and diaries and documents but also from poetry and literature. A discussion of the fur trade in the West should be colored at the least with the words of Jedediah Smith, Black Elk, Washington Irving, and Francis Parkman. Those familiar printed passages drifted from my grasp, and my braille reading speed was not great enough to be effective in a lecture. Luckily, I knew a man with a splendid voice and dramatic talent, my friend Don Stoutenborough, and I talked him into taping passages for me. All

I needed then in class was a portable player and practice in flipping the tape on and off when desired.

Since I also liked to include the drawings and paintings of people who had been on the scene, like Alfred Jacob Miller and Karl Bodmer, it was only a little jump to put the two together into short segments of slides with readings. As it became harder for me to see when to change the slide with the reading, technology leaped to the rescue in the form of tapes with tracks that were cued to the projector.

Before long, I expanded these, too, into double-screen showings with hundreds of slides, lap dissolves, and contemporary music behind the contemporary documents behind the contemporary drawings. The student generation of the seventies was so engaged with music that they loved it when my helpers and I occasionally injected a modern twist from the Beatles or Crosby, Stills, and Nash. For Western hide hunters, we played faintly in the background a bit of "What Have You Killed, Buffalo Bill?" or for a fur trade rendezvous, "Let the Good Times Roll." The more elaborate presentations lasted some twenty minutes and were embedded into the straight lecture material.

These "shows" were woven throughout my two main courses on the American West and California, wherever it seemed that some emotional or artistic dimension was required to fully understand the history—the loneliness of women in the settlement of the plains, the cult of masculinity and violence in the Western hero, the plight of the Donner Party, Chicano displacement following the California conquest. To these more than anything else I attribute awards for good teaching. A colleague, Ron Tobey, called me the Cecil B. DeMille of our department. That was long before Ken Burns used similar techniques to produce his acclaimed Civil War documentary for public television. At least two things, however, separated me from Burns—four million dollars and very milky vision.

Braille was my basic salvation. Oh, Louis Braille, clever man! Like rashes of delight, your crowded pages brought in worlds of ideas and allowed me to let them out again. Half sheets were notes, as they had been earlier in handwriting or typing. I punched braille sheets and assembled them by subject. Binders of summaries with my own notes and thoughts sprouted beside the corresponding books in my library, which were in turn labeled in braille on the spine. For lectures I held the trick of tricks—packs of three-by-five cards with brief braille notes, the structure and ideas of the lecture and specific statistics when needed, tucked in one hand while reading with the other. More deviously, I often buried them in a jacket pocket and let my fingers run over them while I spoke. How memory sharpens with blindness! Caveat emptor!

Another pack of cards identified the students, so I could unexpectedly call them out and ask for comments at any time. Since I asked them to keep the same seats during the term, voice identification was not hard and confirmed the concealed braille cards. The whole system gave me the feeling of being in charge. I think it also kept the students on their toes and minimized their taking advantage of my blindness.

Standard grade-two braille came fairly easily, though no one should think the transition from visual to tactile reading comes without trauma. There are months in which it seems those fingers will never transmit. I abandoned playing the guitar since the calluses were an impediment. Reading prevailed over "The Foggy, Foggy Dew."

For one used to sighted reading, however, braille can never be fast enough. Perhaps that is why it cannot assume the kind of place that sign offers to the deaf. Oliver Sacks claims that sign is the rival of speech, "lending itself equally to the rigorous and the poetic— to philosophical analysis or to making love—indeed, with an ease that is sometimes greater than that of speech." Once learned, sign may be preferred to voices by those who regain their hearing. I found nothing like this in braille. Admittedly, braille may be favored by a person who is blind from birth; then gaining sight means that even the shapes of letters have to be learned as in childhood. But placed on an equal footing with writing and printing, braille is inevitably slower, with no other inherent advantages.

The most important move for me was learning grade-three braille. Grade three is a shorthand version. Most syllables are condensed into one character. Spaces are often eliminated. Sentence capitalization marks are skipped since capitals can be assumed to follow periods. Thousands of words are condensed into one- and two-character symbols. It is a lean and muscular system that pares down a basically cumbersome language. With so many electronic shortcuts available, few blind students learn grade three now, but for me it was a lifesaver.

Subconsciously, I vowed never to become a blind historian without a book, a Homer without a poem, a tin-cup song without a tune. There is more than one technique, however, to writing history when blind, and I capitalized on at least three—braille and recordings, live readers, and eventually, talking computers.

The first problem for a historian is finding his material, and he expects most of that to be in some printed or written form. How much of it will be available to the blind? The basic background works for most subjects are in braille or on phonograph discs and, beginning in the early 1970s, on multitrack slow-playing tapes ($15/16$ inch per second instead of the standard $17/8$). But the general secondary books are not enough for the historian. Documents, obscure journals, and rarer books very soon have to be consulted, and for the blind historian a flesh-and-blood reader is then the only way.

My student readers were a pulsing joy. For my fifteen blind years, they sat across from me, averaging two or three a year, men and women, freshmen and graduate students, conservatives and radicals, serious and lighthearted. Five minutes of hearing them read told me more about their backgrounds than a data bank of vital statistics. How did they handle words like hors d'oeuvres? Achilles? Thucydides? Nietzsche? Goethe? Chartres? Descartes? Edinburgh? Did they stumble or clear their throats over thermodynamics, homosexual, lesbian? When I heard Calvary sound like horse soldiers, I suspected gaps in religion. All grist, and to myself, of course.

Sometimes we drank coffee and chatted. One Iranian student, Reza, brought pistachio nuts that we cracked and ate as we worked. Again it was Mexican sweet bread. I dedicated books to my readers, and I still have a list of their names that I cherish.

Many of these students were supported under the federally financed Work-Study program. They never made much money, but it was a convenient job for them since they could work between classes or toward the end of the day for an hour or two. They were paid for jobs related to their own aims in education. History or political science majors thus read to me historical works, and presumably we both profited. But I suspect there were deeper personal rewards. I know there were for me, as these young men and women gradually relaxed their roles as students and became friends. I rather believe, as some blind writers have suggested, that the sighted reveal themselves more readily to the blind, to people, that is, who cannot see their superficials. In any case, I trust my readers found me less and less the exalted professor and more and more a person they could confide in. Murphy, the paraplegic anthropologist, found something similar happening when his students would touch his arm lightly as they took their leave. Though he remained, as he said, the same middle-aged professorial threat as any other instructor, "they were reaching over a wall and asserting that they were on my side. . . . My physical impairment brought them closer to me because I was less imposing to them socially."

Occasionally, we stormed the archival ramparts. The Huntington Library was the nearest and dearest and had long been to me like manna in the wilderness. I felt that way even when I was introduced to its treasures as an undergraduate, awed by the gilt and crimson of the Ellesmere Chaucer or the haunting, masked face of Shakespeare in the first folio. The library granted me two years of fellowship as a graduate student, and many later summers we moved to San Marino so I could work in its cool retreats. But during my blind years, I was driven over only once or twice a year. Those wonderful librarians gave me a glassed-off, soundproof room where my readers droned over documents and manuscripts and rare books.

One of my readers, John Mack Faragher, went on to become a well-published, prize-winning historian of the American West. Many, taking up their guidebooks in the 1960s, traveled socially radical roads. One, Elizabeth Lopez, became an FBI agent; another, a bank officer. I attended the birth pangs of their careers; they assisted me in course preparation, helped in the grubby spading of history, and cheered my promotions through the academic ranks.

As they read, I clunked away on the braillewriter. These braille notes were topically filed, and from them I wrote outlines, then drafts. When the braille drafts were ready for typing, I transcribed them, a tedious task with hands moving back and forth from the braille page to the typewriter. The typed drafts could be read back for further refinement while I concurrently re-typed, or they could go to a secretary. It was slow, but it worked.

This does not mean that the playing field was wide open. In scholarship, as in any occupation, some subjects, some activities, are more appropriate for the blind. The topic of my dissertation and first book proved to be so. Out of my childhood in the Great Depression I inherited an interest in how societies work, break down, reconstruct themselves. I began mining that preoccupation by looking at utopian ventures in California, describing religious groups like Mormons and Theosophists and socialists at Kaweah and Llano, all seeking better lives. Since these groups tended to be unsung and unrecorded, their archival remains were easy enough on eyesight. But that was happenstance.

Considering what was to come, I would have been wise to keep on in that vein. But, you remember, the curse of Denver lay relegated to some Freudian netherworld. After the publication of *California's Utopian Colonies*, other interests emerged, and I started on another tack—the ways in which ideas are projected in art, most particularly, the influence of art on the images of the American West held by the rest of the world. In the 1960s not many scholars looked at the art of the West, and those who did were collectors and describers rather than analyzers of impact and ideas. William Goetzmann had not yet embarked on his "West of the American Imagination," and Ray Billington had not yet begun his *Land of Savagery, Land of Promise.* I jumped in. Two books emerged—one about Edward Kern, an artist for John Charles Frémont in the 1840s, and another about John Russell Bartlett who drew (in more ways than one) the Mexican boundary after the Mexican war. I never seriously considered the implication of a highly visual subject that required sharp sight for scrutinizing drawings and paintings.

The Guggenheim Foundation did not consider it either, and they sent me for six months to London to burrow in the British Museum for images of the American West, especially by people who had never been there. The grant application was written in the winter of 1966–67, while vision was still reasonably appropriate to the task. By the time the award was granted, some sticky timing arrangements worked out, and the London flight under way, it was April of 1968. That interim was a critical period for my loss of sight. Not even the daffodils were clear by the time we settled down in Pimlico.

But one fulfills commitments. I dutifully sought every painting or drawing made about the American West in every gallery, country estate, or museum in the land. I could make out gross shapes and masses of color. Though my visual equipment reduced many a precise stroke to impressionism, I was smart enough to make adjustments. And Shirley was always by my side, pointing out details. I still have the scrawled, gargantuan notes that I took as we talked over the pictures together.

I was only partially fooling myself. I knew Delacroix and Bonheur and Miller called out for eyes, not for ears. I was on the wrong track. I was Beethoven trying to be a music critic, Franklin Roosevelt aspiring to be a sprinter.

It hit me one rainy day as we descended the pillared steps of the British Museum, hurrying back to our flat where our daughter was holed in, miserable. How much better for Shirley to have been back with her, instead of with me scrounging in my raincoat for the pocket telescope I now used to identify the number of the bus as it came splashing along. The gadget said I had taken the wrong road back in some yellowing wood, and like Robert Frost's diverging ones, not all roads are equal for the blind.

So I forsook Western art and took up a branch of my first subject, the modern extension of communitarianism, the commune movement of the 1960s. If there had been few detailed records of earlier utopias, there were almost none for those thousands of communes springing up like intellectual weeds on the streets of big cities, college towns, and rural crossroads. There were plenty of firsthand accounts to assess, plenty of people to talk to. By the early 1970s, when the communes were burgeoning, my vision was plummeting, but my ears were fine. So off we went to visit the commune world and "see" what was going on.

During these years Shirley and I spent summer after summer visiting communes in the West, nearly a hundred of them. We learned tricks for finding them. Going into a strange town, the best source of information proved to be a health food store. Or along quiet roads, picking up a scruffy hitchhiker could almost always lead us to the gold. "Oh, sure, man, right down this road a piece is Table Mountain, and the turnoff with the red symbol on the left, you know, will take you to Heavenly City." Following directions, we knew, would soon bring into view the collection of broken-down Volkswagens, the domes or tepees, the goats.

Most legitimate communes lived quietly, kept a low profile, shunned publicity, and could not afford sponging visitors. A historian seeking information, however, is not an unwelcome visitor; if nothing else, he reinforces egos. And especially if he comes in his late fifties, has a wife, and, most especially, is blind. The blind are seldom rip-off artists. Then, too, we always bore gifts, usually a big bag of apples or oranges.

We would sit with the communards for hours, tape recorder at our side, talking about their hopes and plans, their successes and failures. Those tapes are still replete with crying babies, mewing cats, bleating goats, and louder music. We listened to ohms, ate tofu, and immersed ourselves in homemade hot tubs, heated with wood fires and filled with naked young people. One very hot day, I walked a dusty trail talking with men and women who had quite naturally and unobtrusively peeled off all their clothes. I remained blissfully innocent of the visual delights. And I once turned down a passing joint of marijuana, not from scruples but because I thought it was a carrot stick. But as in London, Shirley was always there to brief me later.

Thinking of what I missed, I have to admit that even the commune subject, though its documentary hurdles were easily surmountable, raised some barriers for the blind historian. Nevertheless, my results, limited as they might have been regarding nudity and marijuana, appeared in a new edition of *California's Utopian Colonies*.

Perhaps the clearest example of how blindness can change research priorities came in the early 1980s when Richard Etulain asked me to do a volume in his new series of Western biographies. They were to be relatively short books directed at the general reader, and that appealed. My more radical side, again stemming from the Great Depression, frequently wondered why American socialism, in contrast with communitarianism, had so little impact on the American West. A logical target for such understanding was Big Bill Haywood, the one-eyed anarchist Wobbly leader who radicalized the miners of Colorado and Idaho. Etulain's invitation offered a chance to write about Big Bill and perhaps inject some needed radicalism into the generally conservative field of Western history.

For about a year I pursued the subject with diligence. My readers and I delved into the biographies and the secondary material. At the Huntington and the Bancroft, Shirley read the more esoteric stuff to me. Slowly I realized that Haywood was not a good subject for a blind author. He had been dragged constantly into the courts, and there were shelves of transactions in countless cities. The federal government had him on its list of dangerous individuals; Washington, D.C., housed records that detailed his every move almost minute by minute for years at a time. Going through voluminous archives without the possibility of skimming—quickly glancing at a document and moving on, sensing from one heading or one phrase that the manuscript was irrelevant—emerged as a horrendous task. At least, it would have meant relying completely on Shirley, because when one is moving from place to place, it is not easy to corral outside readers.

I abandoned the subject and turned to another in which the manuscripts were amalgamated and the materials manageable. In place of a Western radical, I substituted a Western philosopher, Josiah Royce. One historian-friend, Ted Hinckley, said Haywood was a no-good anyway. And I could rationalize that Royce, the philosopher of community, meshed better with my commune, if not my radical, side. From the standpoint of the blind, he was an ideal subject: at his death his family had obligingly destroyed mountains of his personal papers.

Thus at least twice I was forced to change historical directions. Did that deflection mirror any changes in my general concept of history? Overtly, I went on as before, conscientiously sifting sources, evaluating documents, trying to find at least two unbiased witnesses to prove any fact or event, drawing conclusions based solely on the evidence. I remained, however, like any modern historian, cynically aware that human objectivity is an illusion. In that sense nothing changed.

But since blindness had forced on me a choice of subject, did that not rob me of one level of objectivity? The historian should be able to wander freely amid his data, but the data were being chosen for me. I was not in control. Another filter, another screen stood between me and the truth. There was the rub: the filter had become a part of the truth. The screen was not separating but creating. History had become the same as Clifford Geertz's culture: "the structure of meaning through which men give shape to their experience." I was working now through another culture, the blind culture, which was giving shape to my experience, my historical output.

Blindness would thus seem to have made me a relativist. I had found my own ways of seeing; my reality was not the reality of the sighted. Not just beauty but a whole new gestalt was in the eye of the beholder. I was in danger of becoming a Berkeleyan Idealist. I was prone to saying that the sighted imperialists, believing their way of seeing was superior, did not understand that the "real" world lives in our sensory apparatus. Supplant one sense with another, and reality changes with it. I learned later that Diderot, who had been hailed as the first man to understand the psychology of the blind, speculated on this point even to morality: "How different from ours is the morality of the blind!"

Furthermore, for me now the historical text was in braille when it was not in another's voice, and what did that do to the metaphors and the synecdoches? Remember, my blind years coincided with the rise of deconstructionist theories in criticism, and for deconstructionists, the relationship between the reader and the text is the central quest, quite independent of an author's intentions or the historical backgrounds. I tried to imagine myself face-to-face with another language supporting its own culture of blindness. Could it have some effect, like the linguistic implications of German on Goethe? My words were those of a sighted language (not an unimportant hurdle for the blind), but the visual imagery of those words was lost. Braille differed from print in its conventions, its condensed syllables, its combined words. Those marching dots were formal and uniform without even provision for different fonts. The very word for their single unit was not a letter but a cell. A letter opens up and communicates; a cell confines and imprisons. If Jacques Derrida could create a philosophy around the postcard, what might he do with braille?

I did not succeed, however, in deconstructing braille. It remained for me a tool, not a philosophy. And blindness made me neither a relativist nor a deconstructionist historian. If anything, it reinforced my sense that truth lay in order and system, in the essential unity at the heart of all things. With the blind, order is not presumed or hypothetical; it is proved and pragmatic. For whatever reasons, blindness caused me to turn my back on the divisive Big Bill Haywood and embrace the unifier Josiah Royce.

Royce was a philosopher who would never allow the blind as the weaker partner to accept the lies of their own inferiority. They were part of a lost cause, the lost cause of their blindness, and Royce loved lost causes. They added essential ingredients to his beloved community. As long as the blind understood loyalty to loyalty—an obligation to allow others the same devotion to their own causes—they could never become imperialists like the sighted. The sighted historian assumed his was the only place from which to stand and judge truth. The blind historian found another vantage point. Maybe with will, skill, and humility, the blind historian might begin by recognizing the contradictions, qualifications, and complexities of history and hence be something of a pragmatist. Then he could go on, capitalize on his special experience, and, like Royce, side in the end with unity and absolutism.

Whatever the philosophies I escaped or encoded, the day-to-day job of history consumed most of my attention. And at that level there was always one underlying worry—the corrosive fear that I was slipping slowly behind those fast, nonchalant scholars out there, all those slick models, while I chugged along in a Model T. Clark said it, too: "I can foresee becoming a *mental* cripple and already have fallen into sneaky little ways of covering up for not being on the ball, not having kept up, having missed this and that. It goes in geometric progression." There were times that I wished with her that I had memorized a big dictionary.

Then the computer revolution struck. I first heard of a talking computer late in 1983 at a conference of historians in San Diego. A representative of Maryland Computer Services of Forest Hill, Maryland, let me sit at his ITS (Information Through Speech) terminal, type words, hear them back, and correct my own mistakes. The machine voice was at first hard to understand, but if I struggled, I could get it, and the prospect of editing my own writing without a reader, even printing out in braille or hard copy, was unimaginably exciting. The biggest stumbling block, of course, was the price tag, some $11,448, including the printer and software. That was a lot of money for what might turn out to be no more than an expensive gadget. I called a number of people who used talking computers, especially the ITS. I got nothing but raves for the Maryland system.

Help to purchase came in unexpected forms. The chancellor volunteered some money out of his budget. The dean chipped in. But the largest contributor was the university's retirement system, which reasoned that active work kept me from disability benefits; a few thousand dollars here saved the system a bundle. I put in two thousand dollars, chiefly for the training involved.

So I took up residence with a droning Hungarian who suffered a perpetual cold and lived in my computer box. He became my bonded friend, a flesh and blood Stanislaus. He read to me anything on the screen—letter, word, or line, depending on where the cursor rested and which button I pressed. When I erased a letter or word, he told me what I had done. Visitors from the outside world might not understand him or might be puzzled by his responses; to me he was perfectly clear, a trusted servant and companion.

Sally Wagner, the blind reporter, called her "little guy living in this box beside me" Casper, her Friendly Ghost. She didn't say anything about her Casper having a cold; I suspect her machine was a newer model.

During the blind period, before and after my Hungarian, I wrote three books, some articles, and over twenty book reviews for scholarly journals. The biggest of these projects, *Community on the American Frontier*, came pre-Stanislaus, all braille notes and braille drafts. Stacks of braille for that book covered ranges of tables before we were through. And I say "we" because I envisioned the student readers who fed me the raw material as right there among those stacks; the book was dedicated to them in friendship and gratitude. I longed to see them, those readers so precious to me, but in my mind they were only unfinished shapes of face, figures built of scraps of voice and remarks inadvertently dropped.

I ached to see my completed books and articles when they arrived—the first copies from the publishers, the issues of the journals. These were my intellectual children, but I could only hold them, not pore over their print or pictures, not read the familiar words that through some clanking braillewriter were first born out of me. A printed book is a treasured object for one who can see its typography, spine, and cover and respond to its invitation to browse. True, a new book also has a special smell from new print and a feel, even a sound, to its slightly stuck unopened pages. These latter I appreciated, but I wanted to see the jacket design, its color, its endpapers (if only white), the title page with my name chiseled on it, the clean spaces of meaning that surround the dedication page, the design of chapter heads and initial letters, and everywhere inside, the fonts with which the typographer inscribed my words on his changeless tablets. There is no substitute for the book, certainly not a mechanical tape and not a braille book either, which is too heavy, too bulky, too inhumanly gross to love.

And there is no substitute for a bookstore. Those

aisles of tantalizing covers, the snippet of a poem, an erotic passage discovered, a remembered line in new dress—for me less and less available, more and more an abyss of frustration.

So I knew my readers and my new books were there, but I could not get to them, like a delivery truck on the wrong side of a one-way street and no way to back up. I vacillated, maybe inevitably, from adaptation to frustration. "The lousy thing about 'adjusting,'" as Wagner put it, "is you really never quite know when you're finished." Sometimes the process itself breeds the frustration.

My daughter, Allison, was going through some uneasy early teen years, often distraught and anorexic from her struggle for a ballerina's figure. Arguments, persuasions, tears—we tried and experienced them all.

This is not the place to tell the story of Allison. Suffice it to say that the two of us were embarking on years of real difficulties. How many of her problems were related to my blindness, and vice versa, no one will ever know. In many ways that six months of my Guggenheim year in London proved to be harrowing for us both. I was in the last stages of faint vision, stumbling around, nervously whipping out the pocket scope at bus stops, frequently asking strangers for help or directions that turned out to be painfully obvious. I enjoyed London so much that the difficulties seemed minor. Allison, however, hated the situation and for long periods refused even to leave her little bedroom in our tiny flat. Her recalcitrance infuriated me. We fought, and I do mean fought. The screams of Virginia Woolf could have been no more rending. Who knows what we were really screaming about?

Sometimes my blindness was the cause, she said. Later at home, she left a suicide note (an attempt that failed) requesting that her eyes were to be transplanted to mine when she died. Another time when matters got physical and I had to hold her, struggling, she cried that she could not see into my eyes, could not see beyond that cold white cataract barrier that suggests death rather than life. It was hard to hear her say that. I knew what she meant: the eyes are conduits of expression. Through them flow love and hate, confidence and suspicion, acceptance and condemnation. Without them, how does a child relate to a parent?

Allison's inability to penetrate into her father's expression was but the flip side of what the blind feel. To the blind, no loss can be as great as the dimming of loved faces. There is no substitute for the interchange of a smile. The eye is the only organ that works in two ways, receiving and communicating; no other—neither ear nor skin nor tongue—does both. And when the eye is so involved, it is primarily the face through which it operates. Think of the amount of information we take in through a new face when we meet a person. Think of how much we esteem or deride ourselves because of the way we perceive our own features. When no reflection reveals that face, our very existence is threatened, as with the man in the story who looked in the mirror and saw no face at all.

Mental images remained for all the faces I knew well, though I realized that with the young, in particular, they were swiftly outdated. I knew that Allison was changing fast. My picture was of a fifteen-year-old, when ten years later she was a harried housewife with two children. And her babies, Skye and Christopher, I held but did not see. They were remanded to a world where visual images were blocked while other sensory images drew curtained substitutes—cloudy baby faces lost in space. Holding them did not help much. I was always fearful that I would put a finger in an eye or bend an arm too far or trip while walking with them. I could be nothing more than a marginal grandfather.

And there lay guilt again. Not overt or clear. Clark felt something like that as a young woman when her apartment was condemned and the tenants had to move.

All down the street we began avoiding looking at each other; it was as if we all shared some huge, horrid guilt; I suppose the guilt really was that we were already in training for violating our own memories, wiping out all those years of our lives, because we would dream about them and were afraid of our dreams.

Shirley's face, though, never seemed distant or frustrating. Our lives were too intertwined. I was sure I knew what she looked like; her face was fixed in my mind, and I held to that securely. I realized we were aging. It would have been good to be able to watch us age together. It is important with one you love so much to hold a reciprocal relation of seeing and being seen, wanting to be seen by as well as to see the one you love. And if you cannot see yourself in the way your love is seeing you, a helpless, incomplete feeling intrudes.

It was hard to give up driving. For urban southern Californians, it marks the end of spontaneity. From there on my schedule had to be carefully meshed with someone else's. I was, as Murphy described the paraplegic, a passive recipient, "waiting for the world to come to [me]—in its own time, if at all." I stopped driving at a point just before Thurber did. He described some of his last times at the wheel.

A peril of the night road is that flecks of dust and streaks of bug blood on the windshield look to me often like old admirals in uniform, or crippled apple women, or the front end of barges, and I whirl out of their way, thus going into ditches and fields and up on front lawns, endangering the life of authentic admirals and apple women who may be out on the roads for a breath of air before retiring.

Oh, how I appreciate Thurber's penultimate feelings: "I have a curious desire to cry while driving at night, but so far have conquered that, save for a slight consistent whimpering that I keep up." Not long after, one bids farewell to spontaneity and quits.

I should not whimper, though; life for me was not as gloomy as Thurber's driving. True, I often enough felt with him "like a blindfolded man looking for a black sock on a black carpet." But I don't remember anything like his despair: "I would sell out for 13 cents." I never hit bottom as with Alcoholics Anonymous; never like John Hull "touched the rock" of depression and loneliness. Instead, my signature always tended to scrawl upward from its intended line, like an upbeat flourish. I am told that sudden disability, unlike Thurber's and my slow descent, is more likely to produce discouragement and melancholia and mourning, and in those cases the sadness is only mitigated by a slow realization of positives that surround the negatives.

In fact, for me the prolonged decline included much lightness. I remember when the electricity went off in our offices. It happened several times, and since our building was constructed to house library stacks, there was very little window exposure. Without lights, the inner halls and stairwells were absolutely black. In such an emergency others were thrown into a panic; for me it wasn't that different. The call came echoing down the halls, "Where's Bob? We need him!" And, tapping with my stick, I led the procession, hand in hand, down the halls and stairs to the outer daylight.

Occasionally in the spring on a Friday or Saturday afternoon, the department held a softball game, with the graduate students challenging the faculty and staff. I usually went to the picnic and loved being nominated umpire by the faculty. The students would feign to protest only my faculty status, nothing else.

Quite different was the day of my father's funeral. It was just a few friends in a small chapel. The family filed in from a side door to sit before the casket and the minister. Someone put my hand on the back of a pew, but I thought it was facing the opposite direction and kept trying to sit down back to the casket. My brother Dick simply stepped his 250-pound frame over, lifted me, turned me around, and sat me down right. This started repressed titters, and during the brief ceremony, waves of throttled giggles jiggled our pew. You might guess that I do not have a terribly reverent family.

Our next-door neighbor, Ellie, was a high-spirited widow who openly admitted she was looking for men. At a neighborhood party I went into her bathroom, holding no worries about messing up nice facilities like hers, for I had long learned to sit, not stand, at the toilet. Still in there, however, I knocked a whole stack of paper towels into the wash basin but did not realize it until the water backed up and I felt a bulky, sodden mass. When I called for help, the party got a big laugh. Ellie contended I saw more than I let on. Every one of those dripping paper towels had a nude woman printed on it.

Believe it or not, I started piano lessons, abandoned since a boy. Shirley joined me, and a talented woman, Betty Zuehlke, came every other week to teach us both. With Shirley, she was traditional, rehearsing everything from Czerny to Mozart. With me, she was wholly pragmatic. I wanted lively things, like Scott Joplin. She would painstakingly transcribe onto tape the separate hands with verbal comments—a fifth, a dominant chord, a triplet. We always played in the key of F-sharp, because its first note provided a good anchor on the keyboard. I would learn the parts and eventually put them together. It worked reasonably well, and oh, what a boost for the ego when I played for the neighbors!

There was a strange joy in providing amazement. Identifying others by their voices never ceases to surprise, though only the blind realize how expressive a voice can be, how near it can come to a face in telling emotion, strain, fear. The sighted tend to be astonished when the blind use those clues to their advantage.

Children especially are often baffled by the blind. We were lucky in having across the street a fine family of five children who flowed fairly freely in and out of our place. Chad enjoyed leading me around, or at least I thought he did. And when the craze for Transformer toys swept the juvenile world, the kids twisted their jointed machines into strange shapes and made me guess by feel what they had created. It took imagina-

tion on everyone's part, for the shapes were all hinged
and squarish and disproportionate, but it was fun.

The sighted underestimate the joy of touch. After a
few years of total blindness, Hull at last felt he knew
such delight: "I am developing the art of gazing with
my hands. I like to hold and rehold and go on holding
a beautiful object, absorbing every aspect of it." I have
been in museums where the blind alone are permitted
to finger sculpture. When the Scott Gallery opened at
the Huntington Library, one of the guards, who scru-
pulously warned others, broke the rules and invited me
to touch the Jacob Epstein bust of Albert Einstein. Just
as an eye might explore that bronze head, linger in its
shadows, and understand strength, challenge, independence, and intelligence, so I came to the same
through the feel of pitted metal, wild chiseled hair, fur-
rowed wrinkles, the enormous dimension of that brain-
case.

Without being mawkish or romantic, the gray socks
in me tried to make the best of things. I could noncha-
lantly navigate familiar corridors with only an occa-
sional brush of knuckles along the wall. If sound was
to be my medium, then I would capitalize on sounds.
Shirley identified birds by their feathers, while I would
learn their songs—the birders' Jack Sprat and his wife.

I bought the Audubon Society recordings of bird calls based on the Peterson guide. Over and over I listened to the titmouse and the wren warble to their mates and friends. I tried and tried to whistle back at those records and identify one chirp from another. It never worked. I could appreciate recordings of conversational Spanish and German, but bird calls never became my thing.

The effort was symptomatic, I think, of the way I reacted to blindness. If that was the way it was to be, then that was the way it was to be. My profession not only was good economically but it also became a kind of retreat. The office was so familiar, untouched by anyone but myself. There I could ignore my blindness. There my innate desire to work and do well was rewarded. It satisfied what Arnold Beisser, the disabled psychiatrist, calls the need to live intensely. I could even fantasize that students really cared what I was saying, that someone might actually want to read the books I was writing. Teaching evaluations were good, promotions came on schedule, and book reviews were mildly complimentary. Did I cease wanting my old sight back? Well, at least I stopped thinking much about it. I was perfectly prepared to live out my life, and Shirley was prepared to live it out with me, blind.

Dr. Mueller moved away, and her replacement, Dr. Winters, after a year or so did the same. In 1979 my case was turned over to a doctor whom I would come to worship and whose effect on my life I could not then even remotely imagine. I reported to a new ophthalmologist, Dr. Jeanne Killeen, a delightful, young, Irish woman, married with three children. Eventually I got to know those children through pictures on her desk. But that was not yet. Her voice was worth a ton of medicine; it had a lilt; it was pure smiling confidence.

3

White Canes

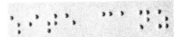

In the 1960s when my vision fell to a corrected 20/200 in the best eye, I was officially blind. That is the definition generally applied in the United States. But I did not accept the condition of blindness. I did not feel blind. I avoided the word. I was skillful in hiding the impairment from others and from myself. I was willing to say that I was having problems with my eyes, or even that I was visually impaired, but long after my vision was far worse than 20/200, the term "blind" was almost impossible to verbalize. As with Andrew Potok, the artist, the word was "fraught with archetypal nightmares: beggars with tin cups, the useless, helpless, hopeless dregs of humanity." When Potok first heard it applied to himself, he wanted to scream.

With the white cane it was the same; there was reluctance, real resistance. For years I did not use that badge of cowardice, when for safety I certainly should have. It is an almost universal reaction. Vajda substituted his umbrella for a dreaded white cane and, when he was forced to the latter, buried the hapless umbrella in his garden with solemn rites. Wagner hated her cane. She called herself "the original klutz" and her cane "a real wash-out." She never mastered the rhythm of her step with the back-and-forth swish. One end caught in cracks while the other jammed into her stomach. The cane did not help when she was lost. And "worst of all," she said, "I might as well have waved a banner advertising my blindness."

In 1975 I fell down a flight of steps and landed on gritty, pitiless brick. They were the steps to a party of friends. It was Thanksgiving time. I was in high spirits, with little thought of my blindness, which was pretty well advanced by then. That morning I had been awarded a National Endowment for the Humanities Senior Fellowship to study community on the American frontier. With the Washington letter in my pocket, I was, shall I say, walking on air, which I literally did. I thought I was at the bottom of the steps, but actually there were three or four left.

After lots of help getting inside and a stiff drink, I

was carted away in an ambulance, thereby completely spoiling the party. I never got to read the National Endowment letter to my friends! The whole event made me gun-shy of good news, and ever after when desires come to pass, I wonder how near tragedy lurks. My hip was broken, requiring surgery, a pin, and months of recovery. Believe it or not, I still found excuses to avoid the white cane.

Another time I was happily letting Chad, a six-year-old neighbor, lead me upstairs to see or hear something in his room. To his horror I missed a step and cascaded down a set of stairs. They were softly carpeted this time, so there were no breaks, though plenty of bruises. Aaron Salinger, a ten-year-old friend, presented me with his treasured twisted-wood cane, but I wasn't reading the real message, even from the rod of Aaron. My pride was beginning to fade, however, and after the second fall, I began using a cane cautiously. I even took mobility instructions. Shirley kept reminding me that a white cane was a protection against misunderstanding, a clarification for all those unreturned smiles, inappreciative stares, blank recognitions. Then some adviser warned that if anything happened to harm me or others in public while I was not carrying a white cane, I was legally responsible. That hit home, and I began to use the infernal stick regularly. But I always understood Potok's cry that with the cane he had become "the stuff of people's nightmares."

One way of looking at blindness is to see it as a partial extinction of ourselves, and we do not generally give up ourselves without a fight. When blindness comes on slowly, the fight is merely prolonged. There is always that bit of light or vaporous form to hang an excuse on. For me the darkness did not crash down in some traumatic accident. It ate away like a shadow in the afternoon and led me to think that little was happening, or at least the problem was not serious. When you can continue to work, teach, and write, as I was doing, why should you admit to yourself that you are blind? I lived in the present, or even the past. Through all my blind years, I continued to wear eyeglasses though they had no effect whatever, and Shirley had to tell me when they got impossibly smudged. I would not go gently into that night, but with a cracked, pinned hip, bruises, an uncontrollable fear of falling down another flight of stairs, and still wearing ridiculously impotent eyeglasses. At long last I brandished a white cane to announce my surrender.

To many blind people, canes and stairs are positives. The cane, of course, is an extension of the arm. It widens the horizon. It is the self, probing the environment by the inch or the foot, just as the eye probes it by the mile. For these blind people the stairway is much less frightening than it might seem. Once on a stair, the next risers are predictable. Rails are usually at hand. Seldom is there litter to trip on. There are no half-opened doors and no head-height obstructions. All these things are true about stairs, but I must admit that I never reached that level of relaxed understanding. Stairs, even the thought of them, always filled me with sinking terror. A cane is a good support, but I never felt it liberating my horizons.

When I entered the white-cane world, I had no concept of the population I was joining. If I had asked, I would have learned that statistics for the blind are not easy to come by anyway. The general reluctance to use white canes is only a symptom of the widespread hesitation to admit blindness; figures can therefore be unreliable. Thousands in the United States do not claim blindness even though their vision has fallen below the legal definition of 20/200. That is why estimates for some years vary from 441,000 to 1,700,000, not including the millions who are functionally blind, unable to read ordinary newsprint with perfectly fitted glasses. I would suggest that the most reliable estimate is that of the National Federation of the Blind, 750,000 blind in 1992. I had joined three-quarters of a million people.

If I had been born elsewhere, my statistical cohorts might have been fewer. Other countries often use far less generous definitions of blindness, sometimes allowing no more vision than the counting of fingers at a distance of one yard. With such narrow definitions, the numbers of blind sink as low as 53 per 100,000 (Germany) or 58 per 100,000 (Switzerland). At the other extreme, in countries like India and Egypt, partly from definition and partly from health conditions, the number can be in excess of 500 per 100,000. The world's blind in the 1970s were estimated anywhere from 14,000,000 to 22,000,000. An even larger figure would be necessary to reflect the sociological or functional definition proposed by the National Federation: "One is blind to the extent that he must devise alternative techniques to do efficiently those things which he would do with sight if he had normal vision." With that definition I would have been blind since I first devised the taped quotations for lecturing.

Not many of the group with whom I was numbered, however, were blind for the same reason. Uveitis is an important but not a leading cause of blindness. In one statistic it accounted for 2.5 percent of the blind; higher, if considering only younger people. It is sometimes related to venereal disease. In some parts of the world, it is especially connected with leprosy and tropical fevers. Everywhere, it is associated with infectious viral and bacterial diseases like tuberculosis and syphilis and not infrequently, as in my case, with rheumatoid arthritis, especially the juvenile variety. The associated diseased cells target parts of the eye, such as the cornea, the sclera, or the uvea.

Very few people have ever heard of the uvea, and one of the hardest situations in the early blind years was explaining my medical condition. I likened the uvea to a thick grape skin running around the outer parts of the eyeball. Actually it is a highly vital structure: one of its parts, the choroid, carries blood through its rich veins to the outer part of the retina, while its ciliary body generates the aqueous humor, the central portion of the eye, the pathway for light, the jelly that maintains proper pressure in the whole eyeball. The uvea also contains the iris, and with that my listeners had no difficulty, especially if I was speaking with my communards. Cultists of the 1960s were convinced that in the iris, secrets of the entire body were revealed. I often wondered what they would have found in the contours and color gradations of my iris as the uveitis took its toll.

I know they would have seen continuing inflammation, which was causing the iris to produce fibrous exudations that clogged up the whole system. That chronic infection led to the usually slow, sometimes rapid, growth of the cataracts. In turn, these were hastened by the use of cortisone, which paradoxically provided the most effective treatment for the inflammation.

The cataracts were easier than the iris to explain. Most everyone knows how cataracts form in the lens, the eye's crystalline prism of a window. Because the lens, like the cornea, is not connected to the blood supply, the cataract will continue to develop until it has clouded the lens sufficiently to be called a mature cataract, which generally means total blindness.

Cataracts allowed me to join a significant subgroup of the sightless, for they are responsible for up to 20 percent of the blind in the developed countries and far more in the Third World. Babies can be born with cataracts as a result of their mothers' illnesses, but every person is apt to develop them with aging. This seems to be the result of the exposure throughout life to ultraviolet light. Cataracts that result from aging are unlike those caused by disease, which are usually posterior and adjacent to the lens capsule.

Most everyone knows, too, that the surgical removal

of cataracts is commonplace and highly successful. From one to one and a half million are removed in America each year, and in the population at large, there are about eight million people who have undergone cataract operations. That striking fact made it hard for others to understand why I stood still and let blindness engulf me. It was at that point that I had to go back and explain the uveitis that blocked the surgery.

My new community of the blind came to their state from causes that were legion. There is a motion blindness in which individuals can see a quiet object but not one that is in action. Ordinary light can produce such pain that a perfectly functional eye is to all intents and purposes blind. Psychological trauma can bring about functional blindness in which people simply refuse to see. Such has been reported for certain Cambodian women now in the United States far from their homeland. In our age of psychologizing, it is inevitable that blindness should be linked with mental problems.

Perhaps the most ironic and melancholy cause, however, came from the oxygen tents in which premature babies were unwittingly placed in the 1940s and 1950s. Some eight thousand children were blinded by this retinopathy of prematurity. One of my blind students, Gary Schmidt, who had an enormous effect on me, lost his sight in that same cruel backlash to medical helpfulness.

Before Gary entered college, his high school counselor, who had heard that I was blind, brought him over for introductions. The young man was shy. It took him months, maybe a year, after my repeated suggestions, to call me Bob instead of Dr. Hine. But his voice spoke enthusiasm; he liked the word "Wow." In the years ahead I created a picture of Gary as tall, well proportioned, agile, with a mop of dark hair over his forehead. He became a friend as well as a student, and before he graduated, we drank hundreds of cups of coffee together and shared innumerable lunches. As he led me to the cafeteria across the campus with his stick tapping, the blind literally leading the blind, his defiant independence made him so quick that I could not keep up and frequently asked him to slow down. He was like Hull, who contends that most help is a hindrance, that all those well-intentioned calls of "Turn right" or "Watch out for that" do little more than make him forget the telephone number he is trying to remember.

Gary's roommates were an active bunch; they cooked special curry dinners for Shirley and me. Once, in his room Shirley noticed his Optacon (a device that translates print into raised needles under a finger), and on it was Alex Comfort's *The Joy of Sex*. I had not read *The Joy of Sex* myself (though the day would come), and it was probably my fault that we did not talk of intimate things like girlfriends. I guess his roommates took care of that subject. But Gary and I were close, and we helped each other. I could advise him, listening to his grand plans for teaching medieval history in college, trying gently to dissuade him from what could be a wrenching goal for the blind. He was more positive, encouraging me to master grade-three braille. When he was home in summertime, we corresponded in grade three and corrected each other's mistakes.

Gary was granted his B.A. with honors and went on to graduate school in medieval history at UCLA. His advisers there were rougher on him than I had been about his prospects in the marketplace, and he only finished one year, returning to Riverside to work in the public schools with blind and handicapped students. He was liked and did a good job and continued in that line in Colorado and later in northern California. I never forgot what his dream had been, however, and blessed my stars that I was functioning as a professor before the sight was taken away.

It always has disturbed me that Gary was denied fulfillment of his ambition. I strongly support the National Federation of the Blind (the preposition is important: *of*, not *for*) in its drive to eliminate such discouragement. The Federation, a civil rights movement that emerged from New Deal days and matured in the era of the Great Society, has railed against sheltered workshops and "broomcorn," restrictions on the blind in air travel, prohibition of guide dogs in restaurants, and in general those sighted attitudes encapsulated in a language that includes phrases like "blind alley." The movement will make certain that the blind never again are "overseen but not heard."

I knew blind college professors, and they had been real successes. Jim Burns, for example, a good friend of Shirley's in college, was blinded at age five by a rare form of glaucoma. When he finished his master's degree in psychology, he sought a teaching job. State law directed that having met all other qualifications, the blind could not be denied a teaching credential, but it said nothing about hiring, and local boards of education often maintained health codes that required teachers to have good sight. Seven years went by, including a period in which Burns vended newspapers and candy at a stand in a state employment building. A psychology professor at Los Angeles City College, infuriated by this derailing of a trained and brilliant mind, challenged Burns to apply for a position for which the health requirement was suspended during a three-year probationary period. Thus began a thirty-year, highly meritorious career teaching psychology there.

I envied Burns his skills. He reads braille faster than anyone I ever knew (up to 150 words per minute, which is about the speed of normal speech). It is a joy to hear him recite while his fingers race over a Thurber story. On the piano he plays Bach and Brahms with verve and warmth. And what a sense of humor! Witness one of his limericks:

> *On the breast of a strumpet named Gale*
> *Was tattooed the price of her sale,*
>   *And on her behind*
>   *For the sake of the blind,*
> *Was the same information in braille.*

Another friend, Werner Marti, a fellow historian, was totally blinded playing high school football. Five years later a social worker helped him get into UCLA. He joined a fraternity, and the brothers challenged him to live as normally as possible and look straight at a voice rather than let his blind eyes waver. As a result, casual acquaintances often did not realize he was blind. He taught at a nearby preparatory school long enough to get himself admitted to graduate school with a teaching assistantship and returned to UCLA for the doctorate. Fortunately, he was directed by a renowned historian-humanitarian, John Caughey. Under him, Marti persisted through the completion of his dissertation on the California conquest, which was published as *Messenger of Destiny*. The doctoral degree, however, led only to years of futile searching for a job. At California Polytechnic Institute, then a small agricultural school in Pomona, three years of application and repeated contacts finally produced a regular position. He taught there very successfully for nearly twenty-one years, nine of them as chairman of the history department.

I do not know John Gwaltney, but he bears the double whammy of being both blind and black. He is a professor of anthropology, who in his book, *The Thrice Shy*, tells of his fieldwork in a small Oaxacan village where blindness is endemic from a local fly-borne disease. He points out that his work is founded not so much on visible as on audible evidence—the emergence and recession of death knells, the crackle of Belgian rifles, the escalation of canine din, the alternations of domestic and imported speech. "The braille-writer, the typewriter, the tape recorder, and a pair of attentive, accessible ears" were the primary resources of his book. His fieldwork in the steep, rocky, stepped Oaxacan terrain wore out six collapsible canes in a month and forced him to use heavy steel sticks.

The blind of that village are a long way from me or any of the academic blind in the United States. For one thing the Oaxacans (poor candidates for the National Federation of the Blind) accept their dependence stoically. Their culture offers them few occupations, except begging for food. The people have a saying, "As poor as a blind man," which implies a great deal. Although modernization is rapidly changing the society, there remains much social deference paid the blind, children are still often expected to act as guides, and there persists a belief that the blind live under special divine protection. The contrast between Gwaltney's own life (and mine) and the culture his culture freed him to study is dramatic.

Robert Russell, totally blind from the age of seven, stocky and strong, a champion wrestler, "a fat little guy, just like a turkey," fought his way through a blind school and a bachelor's degree at Yale University. There he learned to love poetry. With Wordsworth and

Coleridge and Edith Sitwell, his "spirit lay bare in the sunshine of spring." Though his blindness made him feel "like some strange beast tethered by a malignant deity at the gates of paradise," he went on to an M.A. at Yale and then to a B.Litt. at Oxford University. Even with those impressive degrees, jobs came with difficulty, and he spent some time in the mentally deadening tasks of a workshop for the blind, remanded to the broomcorn. After years of countless letters of inquiry and fruitless interviews, he secured a permanent position at Franklin and Marshall College in Pennsylvania. Russell's story, along with all the others, causes me to wonder if I could have made it had I been blind before I was hired.

Still, the blind academic is familiar enough. There are at least six hundred blind teachers in America, according to David Ticchi, whose doctoral dissertation at Harvard was on this subject. At least two leading figures in the National Federation have been university professors—Jacobus ten Broek (California) and Floyd Matson (Hawaii). The evolutionary biologist at the University of California, Davis, Geerat Vermeij, holder of a MacArthur Foundation "genius" fellowship, has been blind since three.

Higher education historically was one of the first areas where the blind were accepted, since student discipline there was a lesser problem than in the elementary and high schools. Frederic Schroeder of the National Association of Blind Educators believes that in the last twenty years, the number of blind in higher education has dropped dramatically. He sees three causes: the greater number of professional opportunities available to the blind, the misplaced fear among hiring committees that the blind might have trouble in the university's frantic priorities of research over teaching, and the lack of training in braille among mainstreamed blind children. Schroeder feels that there are now probably no more than half a hundred blind in higher education.

It is surprising that the television industry created a prime-time situation comedy around this little group. I was peripherally involved in the effort and thought that the day of the blind college professor had dawned. A college friend of mine, Bob Thomas, Hollywood editor for the Associated Press, caught wind of a planned show at ABC called "Mr. Sunshine" about a blind university teacher. Thomas knew the producer, Gene Reynolds ("MASH"). And big names like Henry Winkler (the Fonz) and John Rich ("All in the Family") were involved. Among the actors were equally well-known figures from the theater: Jeffrey Tambor, Nan Martin, and Barbara Babcock.

Thomas told Reynolds of me, a real, blind college professor living nearby. Reynolds called and came out. I expected he might want a minute-by-minute review of my life, the inside story, and since this was Hollywood, even a bit of sexy detail. He must have been disappointed in the latter, but we sat in my office, drank coffee, and talked away a whole morning. Busy as he must have been, he called his secretary to cancel other appointments and stayed for lunch and much of the afternoon. He was interested in my braille cards for lectures, in my class strategy for calling on students, in my braillewriter and talking computer, in the procedure for writing books, in relations with students and colleagues.

I practically memorized the pilot video. The central character, Paul Stark, was like me, having gone blind while a college teacher. But his wife was unable to cope with his infirmity and left him. In his work, however, he did better, successfully understanding students through other than visual means.

Shirley and I studied the pilot carefully, and my commentary to Reynolds went like this:

Slow down Paul Stark's walk and also his reading. A man only two years blind will read braille rather slowly, not as fast as Stark. And when he uses his white stick, his tapping sweeps should be wider and cover his full path. You are right on the mark when you picture him reluctant with his white cane.

I like the show. It is funny, touching, and deals with interesting human questions. You are playing with an idea once expressed by Jonathan Miller (the physician-psychologist-theater man) that we can laugh at the blind because they don't intimidate others. The deaf, in contrast, require others to repeat themselves, talk louder, and feel silly. The blind in their ridiculous stereotype are only themselves made to look silly, bumping into things, shaking the hand of the wrong person, entering a closet instead of the exit, talking to an empty chair.

Since Stark teaches English literature, you might sometime have him lecture on Milton and his blindness, and through his comments on Milton's difficult relations with his wife mirror his own marital problems. I suppose you will in the future capitalize on the widespread feeling that the blind are rejected as sex objects, or on the sighted person's difficulty in imagining sex with the blind.

Finding comedy in infirmity is in itself an enor-
mous contribution. Like most situations in life, the
flip side or the next step in the dialectic can cast a
completely different light on what might be consid-
ered a grim situation. You have explored a lot of
this humor in disability during your career. It
makes us normal. Keep it up.

Sincerely,
Robert Hine

Reynolds asked me to the filming of another episode. On the Paramount set, Shirley and I were seated in the front row of a studio audience. Shirley could not give many clues because of the sound, but, knowing the pilot so well, I could judge the action easily from the words. It was the segment about a blind date (oh, what a hackneyed joke among the blind!). After the show, as the audience applause died down, Tambor came over and shook my hand. I liked his vigorous handshake and his enthusiasm at doing the part. He seemed more than passingly interested in the blind and told me how much he appreciated the help he received from the Braille Institute in Los Angeles. The Hine-Reynolds discussion did not come up.

Because the show was so far along before I got interviewed, I doubt if my contribution crept much into the final eight shootings, but there were a few details that I thought I recognized—some of the relations with the teaching assistants and the unusual uses of braille. In one later episode, the last-minute illness of an actor in a school dramatic production caused Stark to be drafted because he could read his lines from a braille script concealed in his clothing. It was certainly like my pocket lecturing.

Except for its last four letters, I never liked the title "Mr. Sunshine." It suggested Candide's Pangloss, a syrupy message of silver in every blind person's cloud or, equally maudlin, the truly valiant blind conquering their impediment. The show's blurbs also gave that feeling. In them Stark was "a bright acerbic curmudgeon who treats blindness as just another challenge and leaves you laughing." "Mr. Sunshine" was a warm story, well produced and well acted, but the blind are not the raw material for a "MASH" or an "All in the Family." ABC showed the ten episodes through the spring and summer of 1986, but no more were made, and the show quietly died. With it went my day— maybe the day of the blind college professor—in the entertainment world.

4

Movies and Light

Early in my blind years, about 1972, I went to a movie that really hit me, *Butterflies Are Free*. I recognized a kindred soul in Don Baker, a pampered, blind young man. He is determined to make a life for himself despite his handicap, physical and social, and he convinces his protective mother to let him live two months in a San Francisco apartment on his own.

That apartment is a minicosm of the blind world; it is dominated by the blind mind, which imposes a necessary orderliness on chaos. Anything out of place is not only useless but does not exist. On the wrong table the ashtray might as well be on Mars. The sighted world enters that system in the person of Jill, a flighty, nineteen-year-old aspiring actress (played by Goldie Hawn) who lives on the same floor next door. When she first comes into Don's apartment, she cannot get over how orderly he is. If she moves his ashtray, he flicks his ashes on the table. My mind filled with memories—the unwittingly moved glass; the coffee cup crashing to the floor; the misplaced notes never found.

Butterflies was sentimental, admittedly, but it said things I was only beginning to feel in my early days of sightlessness. On a rainy day, for example, Jill suggests they eat potato salad and salami on the floor. Don has a better idea: let's go to the beach. He knows a palm-shaded, uninhabited sandy spot. Where? Over there by the table. You can see it much better if you are blind.

I thought of that conceit when Shirley and I went to the stage version of "Hair." During the famous nude scene, so well advertised, music and imagination created a highly erotic show for me. Shirley said the stage lights were so dim she couldn't see much of anything. My stage lights were on full, in just the right places.

The same impression came in reading Thurber's complaint in a Paris nightclub. "It wasn't until I began to sing with the band about 5 a.m. that I learned there had been a series of strip-tease acts." At least they should have told him, he whined, or they should have taken off $4 from the cost of the champagne. His other solution was permission "to touch the girls as they took their things off." In a London burlesque, David Black-hall, the British civil servant, was greeted with a better phrasing: "Busty, he can't see. Let him check you braillewise." Imagination, run wild!

That was the point of *Butterflies*, as I saw it. Imagination is the key in the competition between the blind and the sighted. Whether or not senses like hearing and touch grow sharper, the ability to imagine must intensify, and it is there that the blind can outshine the seeing.

"Don't be self-conscious about blindness," says Don. "People are always trying to take on the burden of guilt." I knew that my parents had shouldered that burden. I guessed that their unending kindness was working out some deeper unconscious feelings of responsibility. I doubt if they felt, like Jill, that "blind people were kind of spooky," but many do feel that way, and such feelings make it easier to be conscience-stricken or embarrassed. I somehow sensed that I, too, might become "spooky," gifted with shadow vision, searching for voices, purveying guilt tempered with awe.

Jill and Don discover that they, the sighted and the blind, can open an adjoining door. What a metaphor for the two worlds, the dark and the light, separated by only a small opening. She becomes his lover. The light conquers the darkness: he is no longer the unjustly perceived Peeping Tom; she "liberates" him, taking him to funky shops for new clothes. The two are united in sex.

Don's mother—my mother, the outsider beyond admission to the union—discovers their love match and, unable to understand how light and darkness may meet, is appalled. Don seeks independence through the coition of blindness and sight and asks even to be hurt if it takes that to prove his humanity. He knows his Dylan Thomas: "I would not go gentle into that night. I would rage against the dying of the light." And here I was with Shirley beside me in the dark movie house, going so gently into my night.

The story troubled me enough to go (via Talking Book) to the work that had inspired it, blind lawyer Harold Krentz's autobiography, *To Race the Wind.* What interested me there were Krentz's experiences as a blind child, experiences I had totally escaped. Seven-year-old boys would taunt him because he was blind. Girls danced around him singing, "You can't see. You can't see." One mother would not let her child play with Harold because he was blind. As a nine-year-old he had already resolved, "I would not be a blind man in a blind world." Well said, Harold; I'm with you all the way.

Many years later I told a blind woman on the campus

that I felt Krentz had gone overboard with a persecution complex. She refrained from telling me how little I knew, but she frowned and said that to her, Krentz was right on the mark. As a child her nose had been bloodied by a boy calling her blind, and she could tell other stories. Her explanation was that sighted kids get jealous of the blind, seeing the deference paid them and the extra help given them, and so they lash out.

I know now she was right. I have read Russell's descriptions of the "soft ripple of children's laughter" and the "tiny bright fountains of delight" as young persecutors peppered him with green apples. "I was at their mercy and they had no mercy." He felt that others were afraid of blind children and simply did not know how to play with them.

I have heard of blind beggars attacked under the excuse that they are imposters. There is one story, often repeated among the blind, of a policeman mercilessly beating a "blind" man who carried a white cane and at the same time read a newspaper.

"I have a blind mother," yelled the officer to the presumed imposter, until he noticed that the blind man held his paper upside down.

In all these cases the fury exceeds the offense. So I came to realize that when strong and imaginative, the blind, like any other minority faced with rupturing, conflicting social attitudes, must bid vigorously for independence, as did Krentz. Russell counted his deliverance the product of friends who made no allowances for his blindness. For example, he related that one of his pals "assumed I could climb any tree or fence he could climb, and so I did." Friends of that stamp are hard to find.

Movies remained a big part of our lives; we never stopped going. Bodies and gestures and colors on the screen grew less and less distinct, but surrounded with well-spoken dialogue and clever sound effects and with a little ingenuity added, the outcome was not bad. And to be attentive to the background music in movies is to observe emotional manipulation at work. It was fun to infer from the sound track alone the moments of heroism, the rising passions and lusts, the chases, and the mysteries.

We sat apart from others, so Shirley could give me verbal clues. Of course, it did not always work. In *The Gods Must Be Crazy*, on the journey with the Kalahari boy seeking the edge of the earth so he could drop off the infernal Coke bottle, Shirley laughed so constantly she was worthless as a helper. Subtitles raised a formidable barrier. We tried to sit separately with Shirley reading them to me, but it was just too cumbersome. Fittingly, *Z* was the last foreign film we tried. After that we gave up on movies with subtitles.

Stories with little action and lots of talk were the best. *My Dinner with André* was such a gem—a whole evening with two men, the sensualist and the intellectual, talking their hearts out while they ate. I missed the visual experience of the table, but I sensed the food was important and supplied my own crusty capons, bubbling sauces, and crisp asparagus. My menu did not disturb the words as they flowed in ribbons of thought through the quiet theater.

Once by chance in the movie *E.T.*, we sat behind a group of students from the Riverside School for the Deaf. They were there for the visuals; I was there for the sound. They lived in a world of space that they could see and therefore knew directly things that are permanent and unchangeable. I lived more with sounds that came and went. In the theater, space had little meaning for me beyond my seat and Shirley's hand beside me. For the deaf students, it was all space, the dim image of the walls and aisles and the infinite distances projected on the screen. Not so much two kinds of deprivation but two worlds of experience sat back to back in the black box of that movie house.

I found the lucid blind writers were the ones who

understood that distinction. One of the most perceptive is the Frenchman I have already mentioned, Jacques Lusseyran, totally blind from the age of eight. He remembers as a boy other mothers who would not let their children play with him because he was blind. He felt sorry for them, as he did all blind children who under the guise of being protected were not allowed to find their second world of seeing. The greatest danger to a blind child, Lusseyran said, comes from sighted people who imagine that their way of seeing the world is the only one, not listening to the blind child's way, ridiculing his ability to "see." One of Lusseyran's unhappy memories is playing with a blind boy who had been thus made really blind. Lusseyran's "second life" was "a stream of light and joy." He says, "I had found where it flowed and stayed close to it, walking beside its banks. Doors had opened inside me leading into a place of refuge, a cave, and everything that happened to me entered there, echoed and was reflected a thousand times over before it was extinguished."

Blind writers understandably talk almost obsessively about light. But usually their concept is simply opposed to darkness, their "portable darkness." That's the term used by Marie McCoy, whose portable darkness, her "Beast," was dispelled finally by what she calls light. Since McCoy is a classically educated academic

wife, lover of Bartok and the ballet, her ideas are particularly relevant. When she talks about light, she
sounds like Lusseyran, for her light is an inner illu-
mination that she even claims to hear.

In such transposing of the senses McCoy again suggests Lusseyran. In discussing light he often uses
words that imply other senses—the musculature of
walking, the echoing of internal dark caves. And sound
implies voices that must for him become stronger,
more significant, as sharpening tones rise like his
streams of light. Voices gave to Lusseyran the very essence of character, hence his skill at screening men of
the Resistance. The voice must stand for him close to
the light in mystical awareness.

Still, in expressing the separate world of sightlessness, Lusseyran and McCoy are more understandable
to me than the blind Hungarian Londoner, Albert
Vajda, who claims to sense character, usually through
voices but sometimes even before a person speaks.
Vajda describes his intuitions in terms of color: yellow
vibrations come from liars; white, aggressors; blue,
hypocrites; and red, the sincere and decent.

Ved Mehta was for me a far better role model. As a
Hindu, he should be expected to share Lusseyran's
mystical sensations, but Mehta has spent so much of
his grown life outside of India (his multivolume auto-

biography is entitled *Continents of Exile*) that he re-veals in his writing very little of that mystical sense. Blind and separated from his family, he found familiar voices faded quickly from his memory. In Arkansas at a high school for the blind, at Pomona College in California, and finally at Oxford University, Mehta was far more the pragmatic cosmopolite. He found his own way of seeing, sufficient in his case for riding a bicycle through Claremont streets or around Seattle lakes with his girlfriend. Yet his traumatic feelings of inadequacy welled up whenever he realized that he could not tell his girl the color of her dress or how she looked that night.

Another man who involved me was Potok, a passionate New England Polish painter (he has been compared to Josef Albers), a man who reads Kropotkin and revels in Beethoven quartets. He is as unmystical as Mehta and calls himself the kind of person who loves airports—"the danger and coincidence stirred up by movement."

Part of my empathy with Potok was our sharing of the slow approach of blindness, in his case from retinitis pigmentosa, whose genetic propensity is frequently carried in Polish Jews—his inheritance, as he said, of a particular "casserole of chromosomes." The gradual loss of color and form devastated him, probably more than it did me, because he is an artist. We did share some wild therapies. My bee stings were administered orally and rather scientifically. His, however, were direct, the result of a tragicomic involvement with a wild-woman healer in London. In time she loosed hundreds of bees on his head and neck before he cried uncle and admitted defeat.

With a bit of vision left, Potok lived for four months with fourteen others in a rehabilitation center for newly blinded adults in Newton, Massachusetts. One of his instructors, a former sculptor out of an El Greco, craggy and spiritual, called his class "videation," visualizing and conceptualizing unseen things. Like séancers or like Mehta on his bicycle, the students focused undivided attention on an object or an environment. Riveting all their senses and using "sound-shadows," they learned to recognize objects without sight. The old sculptor made them practice color. "Remember color," he would say. "Actively, deliberately recall it. Do mental calisthenics to bring back the bright blue sky, a bowl of lemons, limes, and oranges. Otherwise you'll lose it forever." McCoy applied such tricks to color, "a fugitive thing." On his New England farm, Bill Yates used them to fight the fading. I did, too, and they work.

Potok's story held many messages, but above all, it pinpointed for me the issue of sex with the blind. He tells of one painful night in which a fellow student, his friend Katie, a captivating young woman, returned late, as totally drunk as she was blind. She had only one libidinous thought in mind, and Potok could hear her calling his name as her cane clanked toward his dormitory bed.

My reactions came up from the gut, as true and primitive as if I had met a hungry bear in the woods. I was scared and, God help me, repelled. . . . Not because I had qualms about being with women other than Charlotte. Not because Katie was unattractive. She was soft and round and wonderfully loose. I gulped for breath. I was repelled because she was blind. I wanted to scream with the horror of this revelation. I wanted to punish myself, scratch out my own eyes.

Through the years, as I read, it seemed that this concern was constant. Wagner, for example, tells of one romantic Don Juan:

He'd admitted he'd thought a lot about having a "meaningful relationship" with me (whatever that meant), but, he stammered, he just didn't know how to go about it, "what with er . . . your being . . . ah . . . blind and all. . . . How do you kiss a blind girl anyway?" he sputtered.

"Oh, go strum it on your lute, Lochinvar," was all Wagner could think to herself.

Sheila Hocken, another blind woman, took the burden on herself. "I was blind. Therefore he could not possibly be in love with me."

Russell was more practical, feeling his social inadequacies, like the inability to tell a girl how nice she looked. "If I was ashamed of myself, how despicable I must be in the eyes of a girl."

So there they all were: repulsed, irritated, nonplussed, ashamed. How did I feel? How did I handle feelings of rejection and incapability in sex? First, I must emphasize how much these readings underscored my particular advantages in facing blindness. I was sighted through my first sexual gropings, not like Lusseyran who described his blind childhood sexual explorations solely in terms of touch. I was sighted through adolescence and marriage. Therefore, when blind, sex was a matter of adaptation, doing familiar things, maintaining established patterns, rather than reacting emotionally to the fearfully unfamiliar. As far as I could tell, Shirley never shared any repulsion for the blind remotely like the rejection of Mr. Sunshine's first wife or the punishing reaction of Potok. I want to talk more about this later, for it is not the whole story.

Here, however, I reiterate that sex was only part of my good fortune. If I accepted fate more gently, my occupation may explain it as much as my age. Disability for a college professor is not that of the blinded painter or the paralyzed athlete. University teaching minimized the trauma of sightlessness. While I was blind, my campus office was a haven, not a prison. Colleagues and students actually and metaphorically came to me. I served on statewide committees, such as that for disabled students under Vice-President Ad Brugger. Adjustments, sometimes difficult (witness the attendance at Berkeley meetings), were necessary, but through them all I continued to write and lecture. I rationalized that my insights on history were not seriously compromised by blindness.

At least one constraint of blindness actually suited me. I loved order. I was, indeed, like Don in *Butterflies*. Nothing pleased me more in childhood than, about the age of twelve, being given my own room where I could have things in their place and know where everything was at any time. I liked to parse sentences. I loved to outline. I still make lists and check them off. I am a compulsive recapper of ballpoint pens.

Some would say that such routine is for children and the mature, the two opposite extremes of life. Eric Hoffer, the longshoreman-philosopher of *The True Believer*, said that, and I wonder how much of his thought is related to his experience with blindness (he was sightless for ten years from the age of five to fifteen). It is the adolescent, he wrote, "who has lost the child's capacity for concentration and is without the inner resources of the mature, [and who] needs excitement and novelty to stave off boredom." In his adolescence Hoffer regained his sight.

Then Hoffer could take up that chaos which breeds life, as Henry Adams put it, turning his back on order, which breeds only routine. When Adams wrote that, he was neither young nor blind, but the crusty old New Englander, who should have known something about order, could unwittingly have spoken for the blind. Like most of them, I suspect, I felt something disquieting about my ordered life. The advantage that organization provided for me housed its dark side—the brooding uneasiness that the requisite order breeds habit and that habit blocks creativity. One could survive blindness, adapt very well, but never again be a free, creative spirit. There was the rub; there was the worry.

If I felt that way, think how much harder for the adolescent blind to feel Hoffer's "excitement and novelty." I know a woman, Judith Zaragoza, blinded just before her teens and now in her twenties, who says that what she misses most is spontaneity, jumping in a car when you feel like it, taking off for the beach, or wherever, on the spur of the moment. The orderliness of blind life cautions against it, says no.

Thus the older person or one who is by nature orderly falls more easily into the familiar and the routine indispensable to sightlessness. It did not take me long to realize that anything not put where it belonged was chaotically lost and then to generalize that organization, like imagination, would give me at least half a chance to compete with the sighted. As Hull put it, "Familiarity, predictability, the same objects, the same people, the same routes, the same movements of the hand in order to locate this or that: take these away, and the blind person is transported back into the infantile state where one simply does not know how to handle the world."

So, the free-flowing blind person feels a danger, this constant shadow of a world where the "hard-won balance between trust and fear threatens to be upset." For me, much of the time that threat was minimal because I was weird enough to enjoy being organized, and the new world did not too much impinge on my desires, even my desire for sex. If I could conquer blindness by organization, I would do it, step by step. The process itself was victory. Of course, given the choice, I would prefer my organization with sight. "Dark is a long way," as Dylan Thomas said, and I never will deny the blackness and the sadness. I am not a Stoic or a Christian Scientist. But blind is one way to live, and creative or not, I would live.

5

The Last Days of the Cataract

I was working at my desk, listening to my muffled Hungarian read from the computer screen, when a nurse from Kaiser called to say that it was time for an eye checkup and she had a cancellation the following day. For a Kaiser nurse to initiate an appointment was highly unusual, in fact, unique in my experience. But I didn't think much about it. The time happened to be good, and Shirley was free, so we went, expecting only the usual ritual that I had known for so long.

The examination started routinely enough, but when Dr. Killeen came to the pressure reading (Dr. Mueller's "scales" had given way years before to a sonic tonometer), something was not routine. The pressure in my right eye had risen to 32 (10-20 is the normal range). Glaucoma is always a worry in long-term use of cortisone, but something more than that seemed to be happening. The mature, ripe cataract was leaking, clogging up the system, and causing the pressure to build into a secondary glaucoma.

"That old, tangled matter of surgery is no longer a question," she announced with determined gravity. "We must operate as soon as possible."

First, however, the pressure had to be reduced with medication. For a week, therefore, I dropped in Betagan and brought down the reading from 32 to 18. That was a week of fear. For the first time in all those years since Denver, unexpressed, poorly formulated questions began to lurk like phantom wolves. What happens with failure? What if the eyeball must be removed? How do you handle a glass eye? Does it hurt? Do you take it out at night? Do you live in a blackness deeper than my gray?

On Tuesday morning, March 25, 1986, I reported for surgery. Without breakfast and with only sips of water, the admission procedures seemed endless, and there were further delays caused by some emergency in the operating room.

About noon, stretched on a hospital bed, I was sedated and given more eyedrops to control the pressure. An intravenous needle was inserted in my arm, and an anesthetist and a nurse by the name of Mary with a soft southern accent rolled me to surgery. The anesthetist administered a stronger sedative through the IV, and Mary scrubbed my face with solutions. Everything was upbeat, as if this event had transpired a thousand times before, as it had. I thought of little except the operation ahead, whatever the pleasantries I uttered, but the nurses and orderlies chatted about the world outside. Mary, it seemed, coached a Little League baseball team, and we heard all about it.

Electrocardiogram terminals were attached and activated. An oxygen device was inserted in my nostrils. A blood pressure monitor inflated automatically on my arm every few minutes, pumping up and down through the whole procedure like a reassuring friend. Dr. Killeen came in. I could not mistake her musical voice. I tried to imagine her in a surgical mask, her hair bound up in a puffy, white cap. She talked cheerfully, anesthetized the area around the eye with a facial block, and attached the eyelids to bridal sutures that held them open. She told me she was swinging the great microscope into place, and then she began her work, cutting that first tiny incision in the conjunctiva and sclera and then opening the capsule itself.

I felt little or no pain. Which is not to say it was pleasant, for touching the eye is naturally traumatic, even when you are used to it, and the prospect of cutting into that little orb, the heart of our senses—well, I think of nothing less unnerving than castration. But aside from the psychological trauma, the actual sensed experience was quite different.

I saw a field of pure, intense blue, a wild, bright, electric blue, in which white lights vibrated like dancing electrons. Sometimes they would intersect with lines and arcs of light. They were Matisse and Klee and Albers, transformed into kinetic art, alive and magnified into a kaleidoscope revolving around a profound, pulsing indigo. It was how I imagine the LSD experience.

I remember saying, "The light show alone is worth the price of admission." As if from far away, Dr. Killeen answered, "Good." And I had the warm feeling that she was listening to me and that what I was seeing portended well.

Her job, of course, was the emulsification of all that old cataract, irrigating the area, and sucking it out with an aspiration tip.

Then I heard her say to her assistant, "I'm going to do a capsulotomy."

My spirits plummeted. All I could think of was a lobotomy, and the idea of something being excised ricocheted around my mind. I worried that she was encountering more than planned, that something unexpected had been forced on her. If this was part of the original plan, she would have mentioned it to me, or at least she would not need to state it in the midst of the operation. Was the whole capsule coming out, as in an appendectomy? How much of the eye was involved?

When Vajda underwent a similar operation and overheard his surgeon's comments on increasing the incision in the conjunctiva, he quietly panicked.

It is not a piece of sausage, my conjunctive, even if I have no idea what it is, and I shall need all I can keep! It is part of my eye, my private property. I won't give away a thousandth of an inch more than absolutely necessary.

But for me, worry was proving its parentage in ignorance. Once all of that cottage cheese sludge had been removed, Dr. Killeen found, not unexpectedly in such cases of long inflammation, that the capsule wall itself was heavily coated with plaque. In some cases a surgeon will try to clean off the surface, but damage can be done in the process, making it impossible to insert the posterior lens. Other times the problem is postponed for later treatment with lasers. But Dr. Killeen, since she was surgically there, decided instead to make a small insertion in the wall of the capsule, a vitrectomy, to allow light to pass freely.

Dr. Killeen's next task, maybe the happiest of all in the long run and a technique that was little used only ten years earlier, was the implantation of an intraocular lens. The measurements had been taken. It was to be a posterior lens, behind the iris. She re-formed the chamber with a viscal elastic and inserted the lens through a "shooter," into which the tiny device was folded until the proper position was reached. It was then literally ejected, its loops flying out to lock the lens in place.

Finally, the incisions had to be closed. The normal initial incision is about four millimeters and involves one or two stitches. Mine was unusually large and required fourteen. Dr. Killeen used nylon sutures that need not be removed. They would ultimately offer an advantage, for they could be plucked selectively and thereby reshape the eyeball to correct astigmatism.

So, the lens securely in its niche and the fourteen stitches tied, the dancing lights dimmed and the electric blue faded. It was all over in half an hour. But for me, it was both forever and an instant. Time is for the active and the willful. To those abjectly controlled by surgeons and drugs and machines, time is suspended, meaningless.

Sometime, however, Dr. Killeen said, "Mr. Hine, your cataract is removed," and I detected a certain jubilance in her voice. All the phantom nightmares of castrations, lobotomies, and glass eyeballs dissolved into a warm tub of relief. Thick pads of bandage were applied over the eye, but I did not care; they made me no more blind than before.

In a little recovery room with other patients in various stages of animation, Dr. Killeen reassured me again and left me to doze, peacefully. Mary gave me hot soup and apple juice, nectar of the gods, through straws. One by one the monitors for blood pressure and EKG were removed, and, after an hour of rest, I was wheeled out to Shirley and the car. We were home by four in the afternoon.

Hope, however, like the creativity of the blind Milton, has a way of being "swallowed up and lost in the wide womb of uncreated night." This night after surgery was no exception, as I lay on my back, trying not to roll on the left side and disturb the bandage and the operation. I was told there was no danger in motion, but maybe it wasn't completely illogical to keep one's head immobile as my father did with sandbags after his cataract surgery twenty years before.

Morning was better. Except for avoiding the huge bandage, I went through all the familiar routines of washing, shaving, and breakfast. There were family telephone calls before the rates went up at eight, and then, out of the blue, came a long-distance call from the *Journal of American History*. Its editor in charge of television wanted me to review a documentary scheduled for mid-April about George Armstrong Custer based on Evan Connell's *Son of the Morning Star*. I do not know what the editor had in mind asking a blind man to review a visual medium, but I turned him down. At home, however, unknown to the caller, I was pleased. Was it not a marvelous augury that, still in bandages from eye surgery, I was asked to evaluate a television program? I may not review that program, but maybe I would see it!

How could I know that this morning was the beginning of my Day One?

About 10:00 A.M., I sat in Dr. Killeen's office. Even that soon, the time had come to remove the bandages. Pat, a confident, friendly nurse whom I got to know well, did the job, peeling off the tape and pads. When the last one came away, I was looking square at her. And I saw her—or saw a cloudy image in a trousered white uniform. She moved away from me and worked with her instruments; to me, her gestures were exaggerated like a mime artist's. I thought of television pictures of men landing on the moon, walking without gravity, grainy from a million miles.

But all this was almost instantaneous, for then I turned to the one person I most wanted to see again, Shirley, and there was her silver hair shining, her loving face and eyes smiling. She did not seem much changed to me. I guess I had been too close to her during those blind years to let her image slip away, rehearsing it with every joint experience, refusing to let her visually escape. Her hair was white, but it had always been very blond. After fifteen years, her face still glowed with that warm softness that I could see even without touching. Now she was draped in color, wearing—was it deliberate?—a multicolored blouse with wide stripes; I touched the colors and identified for her the yellow, the blue, the green.

Dr. Killeen examined the eye and was optimistic. She found the retina, invisible for so long because of the dense cataract, relatively undamaged and intact. She could find no uveitis activity. The pressure was now only 10.

All the while my eyes looked out over a new fairyland. The examination room was delightful—the counters of intense yellow, the bottles of clear glass and colored labels, the black-handled, silver-edged, glittering instruments. My sight was jammed with the adjectives in my mind.

The drive home rivaled a Disneyland ride or an early Cinerama movie. Cars in unbelievable colors streaked by at breakneck speed in every direction, terrifyingly close. The lines in the street came up like a Mondrian painting—yellow and white, single and double, crosshatched at the intersections, broken or swerving off for a left turn, bent into arrows sometimes multiheaded like hydras. Fifteen years ago the highways were marked simply; now they were dowagers of crowfootedness.

We turned from the towering palms of Victoria onto Mangrove and into our driveway and the garage. It was the first time I had seen our house; we had bought it only eight years ago. The garage hit me first, the shelves of old magazines, the boxes of material, some closed and labeled, some overflowing with junk, the benches with cleaning fluid, tools, wire. Shirley and I are proverbial packrats, and our garage is always a jumble. To me now it was a riot of color and pattern, truly appealing, truly exciting.

In the months ahead I wondered much about sight and beauty. A child can see, but can he or she tell us what is beautiful? Today I became a child again. I saw nothing shabby, nothing gaudy; everything was wondrous. Even our junk-filled garage revealed marvelous forms and patterns and colors. Some kinds of critical judgment may require vision, but they also demand time and experience. On that day I was the lord of childhood and the critic of nothing.

I walked on into our bedroom. It was shadowed with a dark rust carpet, and beyond the sliding doors was the cool, green patio with blue and orange birds of paradise in bloom. Now it was time for tears. It was too much. I cried. Shirley cried. We were supposed to start a series of drops in the eye when we got home, but it proved useless for a while; the tears washed them right away.

The telephone began ringing and hardly stopped for two days. My brother, Dick, called. When he heard the news, there was silence for a bit, and he said hoarsely he'd have to call back after he got his act together.

I could not eat lunch. I felt dizzy and nauseated. After a nap, I was better.

Welling within me was a devotion to Dr. Killeen. I thought how she must feel akin to the gods to give such second sight. She may have done it often, but I was sure it could never become routine for her.

Years later I came across a book by an Englishwoman who went through this experience and shared my feelings. Sheila Hocken was part of a Nottingham family of people blind from congenital cataracts and undeveloped retinas. By the age of nineteen she had no sight whatever but adapted to an Avon sales route by means of her guide dog. Some years after her marriage, a doctor offered to operate, and she took the chance. When the bandages were removed, she remembered,

There was white in front of me, a dazzling white that I could hardly bear to take in, a vivid blue that I had never thought possible. It was fantastic, marvelous, incredible. It was like the beginning of the world.

Unknown to each other, Hocken and I are soulmates. We have shared so many experiences. Newly sensed sunshine and green grass, first pictures from the car window "rotating past . . . like an enormous merry-go-round," the traffic lines ("Don, look. There are all sorts of white lines along the road"), the unforgettable return to a previously unseen home.

I know now of much that I escaped. The psychological trauma, for one thing, can be enormous, a fact that it is not easy for the sighted to understand. By no means all of the blind return to sight happily. Postoperative depression is frequent.

There is one case studied by psychologist Alberto Valvo and identified only as HS, a highly intelligent, well-educated young man blinded in a chemical explosion at the age of fifteen. Twenty-two years later surgery restored his sight. Before his operation, psychological and emotional testing confirmed his complete normality. From HS's diary:

About a month after the operation I began to feel depressed. I still often have fits of crying. I don't know why, unless perhaps because I have seen too much during the day. . . . This is too long and unhappy a road, leading one into a strange world. I may even have been happier before this; now I seem weak, and I am often seized by a great feeling of fatigue.

Such depressive states happen to a majority of persons recovering after many years of blindness. Physiological changes occur as the retina and nerves slowly begin to function again. The patient starts to realize that he must work at organizing his new sense impressions and that he is now considered a sighted person on whom heavier demands will be made. As Valvo generalizes, "The patient becomes depressed once he starts to miss this halo of admiration and popularity; he becomes moody and irritable, and tires easily. . . . His prior intolerable condition of blindness becomes a desirable state of peace and security in which he would like to take refuge." And to these fundamentals are added the disappointments of the seen compared with the previously imagined. Not necessarily contradictory, either, are ranklings at how much one has missed during the years of blindness.

Reading these accounts touched me. I shared all of the basic facts—the physiological changes, the heavier demands, the lost security, the potential disappointments—but not the consequent moodiness or depression. Perhaps my gray socks insulated me from the hazards. Mostly, however, I related to this entry in HS's diary: "I suffered most from an obscure feeling that in my life something existential had occurred and I remember a similar feeling after the death of my father, like a feeling of destiny." I, too, had felt the earth turn.

The first evening of my second sight, Don Stoutenborough, old friend and voice of the blind years, stopped by for the news of the operation. He is a man of deep emotion. With drama in his soul, he suggested we walk outside, and there was the full rising moon. I could not yet make out stars, but the moon was a golden disk, so exquisite, and no one in the hemisphere looked on it tonight with more joy, more reverence.

Don had once quoted to me a poem by blind Argentinian poet Jorge Luis Borges: "the very final rose that Milton held before his face, but could not see":

> *Oro, sangre o marfil o tenebrosa*
> *Como en sus manos, invisible rosa.*

The unseen rose, the once invisible moon, lay now unveiled, and Don, too, had trouble with the tears.

6

Second Sight

Nothing so exciting ever happened to me before, though what it meant was still far from clear. It appeared that I had lost my blind self, but what would take its place? That confident man who had so long kept the Denver prophecy at bay? That dim-visioned person groping around in the early 1970s? A normal individual, fully sighted, loving his wife, seeing his daughter and grandsons, driving his own car? The latter was the royal flush, a little too much to hope for. Whichever, the historian in me emerged. I wanted to document the change step by step wherever it led. I determined to preserve for myself the thrill of these moments. I would keep a journal, and at my braille-writer the day following removal of the bandages, I started the pages that are transcribed below.

THURSDAY, MARCH 27. *The kitchen cupboards as I opened them this morning were like jewel cases. The milk of magnesia bottle was so blue. The Pero carton from which for years I dipped so many spoonfuls and assumed to be beige was orange and saffron with a big "PERO" which I could read! The stove and countertops were, surprisingly, green. I never imagined them that color.*

In the afternoon I saw even better. In a photograph on the bedroom wall, I made out the face of Skye [my three-year-old grandson]. The face of Nona Bess [Shirley's sister staying with us at the time] is filling in, just as Shirley's is doing. I can see the bright blue of Shirley's eyes now, unchanged through the years. In room after room pictures on the wall—like the three Yale prints above my desk and the little "tiger" painting we bought in London—were wonderful rediscoveries. Ellie brought her first garden rose—Brandy it was called, with a dark center spreading into yellow. She came over three times, each time wearing a different blouse so I could identify new colors. The transparent ruby redness of my toothbrush hit me since I had thought it white. My shirts, especially a plaid one, were wonderful, as was the jagged whiteness of a Kleenex coming up toward my face.

GOOD FRIDAY, MARCH 28. *I had an appointment with Dr. Killeen. Vision turned foggy on the way over, but in the examining room I saw a fuzzy "E" at the top of the eye chart. When the pinhole was held up, I could guess at the "S-L" on the second line. The doctor was relaxed and pleased. She found no iritis flaring up. The retina continued to look good. Pressure was 13. She said with this start the vision would get much better. I asked if I could hope for something like 20/80, and she said maybe better than that, perhaps even to the point of daytime driving.*

Tonight at nine o'clock we watched the premiere of "Mr. Sunshine" on ABC. It was the same episode that Gene Reynolds sent while interviewing me as a blind professor. The lines were so familiar, but now for the first time I saw the action, saw Jeffrey Tambor with his beard, noticed the improbable speed with which he covered strange distances (confirming Shirley's earlier observation).

SATURDAY, MARCH 29. *This morning Shirley read me the Riverside* Press-Enterprise *story, "New Ray of Light for a 'Sunshine' Fan."*

"Mr. Sunshine" had a special fan last night. His name is Robert V. Hine and that new ABC series is the first television show he had really seen in 20 years. . . .

I couldn't read the newsprint, but I could see my picture, an old one, and I looked dismally blind.

Some continuing amazements: milk or wine pouring into a glass; the jet of water from the kitchen faucet; the glow of the whole house in the morning with the back patio so green and secluded. I told Shirley that I liked this house; let's buy it. It surely was a different place than the one for which I scrawled a migratory signature on an escrow ten years ago.

How different to play the piano with sight. Pieces I had learned while blind are hard, as if the hands before me get in the way. I find the same feeling when I go now to the braillewriter, the sight of the jumping fingers making the same distraction. Perhaps while blind, the music and the words communicate more directly with the brain and the instrument.

It did not take many days for the hands and the eyes to become more related, and a real freedom in playing the piano followed. No longer tied to fixed positions like the middle F-sharp, I soon found any note by sight. Improvisation became a special joy. I was free to roam. The keyboard was like the whole world. My eyes were able to take it all in, and it was all mine again.

Larry and Lois came down. They seemed trim in body. Lois had a stronger face and Larry shorter hair than my image. They offered "congratulations," the same word I keep getting by phone and on cards. Since I have done nothing, the word is at best inaccurate. I suppose people just don't know what to say. They're obviously expressing relief that such an unambiguous happiness is still around. Sometimes they say "Good news," complete unadulterated good news. In a militarized world, racially suspicious, and morally ambiguous, one person's restored sight takes on the color of unalloyed good.

At breakfast I saw two of my own books for the first time—the community book and the new edition of the Kern. No print comes through yet, but the old Kern pictures, like Edward Kern's portrait, came back in a rush. I love the big illustrations in the community book, but smaller ones are still hard to make out. The jacket lettering is too faint to see, but the design and color of the covers are gorgeous and exciting.

EASTER DAY, MARCH 30. *I wrapped my white cane with spiraled bright blue ribbon, which I carefully chose from Shirley's sewing supply. It was the same color I saw during surgery behind the show of lights. The Graebners joined us, and we all went to St.*

George's [our small Episcopal church near the campus, which we had joined during my blindness]. The interior was warmer and richer than I had imagined—the beams converging over the altar, the altar itself standing far forward, banners ranged on the walls, the choir stationed to the rear of the altar and organ. News of my good fortune had spread. The Bulletin *and the prayers of the people both included thanks for the restoration of my sight. Father [Allan] Chalfant talked with me as we came in. He picked up on my comment that the most exciting part of new vision was not colors or cars but the faces of friends I had never seen. He repeated the idea in his informal comments before the homily.*

Mary Burton was among those who came up. Her blindness raised the disturbing question of who had been chosen. I said something weak about hope, and she responded in a loud voice that her doctor long ago told her there was none. I watched her throw back her head and walk proudly on.

In the press of friends after the service I was struck by the beard of Joel Reynolds and the roundness of Tom Pelzel (whom I had imagined drawn and aesthetic-looking). But mostly I was fascinated by faces, by so much change in the once-familiar ones.

Faces are almost frightening to me, though. Not all details are there, so I see a mouth without lips and whites of eyes without eyelashes. When the light is strong, as it was this morning outside the church, a face seems harsh, exaggerated, like a caricature. I think I tend to interpret this quality as advancing age in my friends. In time I may find that fifteen years have not aged them as much as I think.

This early distorted vision came back to me not long afterward in the lesson from the Gospel of Mark when Christ healed the blind man at Bethesda. After the first laying on of hands, the Bethesdan beheld people "as trees walking." It was only on the second ministration that he "saw every man clearly." I was still in the first ministration stage. But the faces I initially saw were not minimal, not an oval with a line for a mouth and a circle for an eye like a Thurber cartoon. They were grotesque, more like trees walking; there were no teeth, or the teeth were exaggerated; nostrils were like manholes. I remember a phrase from Milton, "day's garish eye." Many of the images of my first days had that garish quality to them. Fortunately, this strange repulsiveness did not last long, and the faces of friends grew daily clearer, more as remembered.

Faces raise so many questions. We assume that the face is the primary means of human contact. "Face-to-face" is a basic term in the language. In the literature of community that I studied so long, it refers to one-on-one relationships, fundamental in the building of strong traditional communities. What then for the blind? Because they do not see faces, are they excluded from community? Obviously not. The blind do not need to "face" one another (though they often do so, turning toward the voice as a gesture of respect or an effort to conform). Theirs is a special bonding based either on their own internal images from voices or on some spiritual sense. Though faces are newly precious to me, for myself or for my community, I realize that the blind have their own form of face-to-face relationships.

Outside of church Shirley bought a cymbidium being sold for some cause. Then the altar guild thrust an Easter lily into her hands and one into mine. The house is now full of flowers. We have Easter lilies, a potted red tulip plant, a spring basket sent by Kevin and Debbie, and roses from Phoebe's garden.

MONDAY, MARCH 31. *4:30 and 6:00 A.M. had pain running through the eye but not lasting long. I noticed that as I lay with the protective patch over the eye at night, the floating areas of cloud that normally move across in imagination were no longer white or gray but were alternating colors—reds or blues, greens or yellows, or mixed. It is as if the mind is savoring its new delights.*

As I close my eyes, I also keep noticing animation. Little figures hop around like Keystone cops, wildly gesticulating with their arms, their heads and faces contorting, as they cavort through the fields of color. These are very vivid and they tend to come just before I go to sleep or am waking up.

The floating fields must be related to the sudden intake of color in the visual system, so long robbed of it. Valvo's patient, HS, experienced them in such a way: "I would see visions periodically of colored crystal and mosaic bits, displaced in perfect symmetry." But they are not simply the result of the new color vision, for some blind people also experience them, and for them it is not a visual impact but a recurrent memory. My blind student-friend Judith saw them. Thurber called them his "holy visitations," an agitated "flux of colors very similar to some of the paintings of Braque." Hull described them as "a round area of fan-shaped pink or light orange light [rolling] around the 'visual field.'"

Of course, Hull, who enjoyed an intense imagination, also enjoyed Technicolor dreams that he felt were escapes from the condition of his blindness, similar to relived memories. "Every time I return to consciousness," he wrote, "I lose my sight again." Apparently color in dreams must be a personal matter. For me, dream color along with these color fields returned only with regained sight.

As for the animation, the psychological literature on restored sight is full of such apparitions. On waking in the morning, HS said he would "see before me, as in a dream, everything I had seen before during the previous day." Valvo describes this phenomenon as a "hallucinatory recapitulation of new visual experiences." Other psychologists differentiate between three kinds of hallucination: simple, like sparkles; geometric squares and circles; and structured figures. At various times during and after surgery, I knew all of these. Since they decrease over time, Valvo concludes that they represent "a process as if a mental stock of images of which the patient had been deprived for years was replenishing itself."

In the morning Aunty and Patty drove out. They each deliberately wore bright colors—Patty red, Aunty teal green. Aunty looks wonderful to me, still using her cane but not much needing it. Patty seems grayer, but her face is not as thin and drawn as I remember it. Good to see her smile once more and the way she tilts her head. I walked with them through the house, showing what I could see anew, like the petit point pillow and scarves Aunty made for us a few years ago, the cloisonné lamps she gave us when we moved into this house, and the little pouch Patty sewed at Christmas. When they left after lunch, Patty looked Nona Bess squarely in the eye and said, "I like you. You're neat." I think everyone just feels good.

Surprising revelations of this day: the swirl of suds in dish rinsewater and their eager unification going down the drain; filling cups without using a finger to test the rim; the picture of Dharmanand [our daughter's husband] with his older face and heavy beard; Phoebe's youth and gestures; the colorful covers of magazines like US News, which when I was last seeing were drab; sweeping the walk and directing the broom precisely where I want it to go; spooning out a grapefruit, segment by segment; buttering my own roll with exactly as much as I want; and knowing where things are on the plate. Gone are the days of "peas at six o'clock, potatoes at nine." In fifteen years how many pats of butter have I forked by mistake, swallowed, and then pretended that nothing was wrong.

These comments recall Hull's association of desire with the visual image of what satisfies it. Hunger soon gets translated into specific food; the sight of food can even create hunger. Thus blind people like Hull can become bored by dinner and lose interest in food. The butter and grapefruit mentioned above reflect some of my restored joy in eating, a reconnection of the visual image with desire.

TUESDAY, APRIL 1. *Farewell to Nona Bess. Shirley and I are now on our own. We know we have a lot of adapting ahead. I notice how hard it is for Shirley to refrain from taking my hand for help at a curb. She reaches out, then looks at me for reassurance that I can and want to do it myself. I have caught her describing a picture instead of just handing it to me.*

When blind, I often rehearsed poetry in my mind. As with light and color, this was one way to hang on to the past. During one of those first sleepless nights after surgery, "Sailing to Byzantium" came up, but it gradually metamorphosed into something else. A few days later, I sent the results to Dr. Killeen:

April 2, 1986

Dear Dr. Killeen:

I hope you like the poetry of that wonderful Irishman William Butler Yeats? If so, you might remember these lines:

> Once out of nature I shall never take
> My bodily form from any natural thing,
> But such a form as Grecian goldsmiths make
> Of hammered gold and gold enameling,
> To keep a drowsy emperor awake,
> Or set upon a golden bough and sing
> To lords and ladies of Byzantium
> Of what is past or passing or to come.

Last night, lying awake, I revised that poem, and I think of it as for you:

SAILING HOME
(following my intraocular lens implant)

> When I shall die, I hope with me to take,
> Not bodily form or any natural thing,
> But such a form as opthal surgeons make,
> A plastic lens of honed enameling,
> To make a sleeping retina awake,

Or, set beneath a trembling lid, to bring
To all the blind deprived of heavenly light,
For all their days to come, a second sight.

With endless and deepest gratitude,

Robert Hine

7

Returns

A fully sighted person might wonder what I was crowing about. I had only one eye, and the vision in that eye was less than when Shirley and I were married. Though it had improved greatly since the first week after surgery, when it was 20/400, it was now not even 20/100. I could not drive. I could not read a newspaper. Night vision was wildly fractured. Headlights were doubled, with one set starting far apart from the other and drawing together as they approached. My journal seemed blissfully oblivious of those details. How long would it take for me to realize that I was not yet ready to conquer the sighted world, and maybe I never would be.

APRIL 1. *This morning Shirley drove me back to the campus. What an experience to turn from Pennsylva-*

nia Avenue and see those green and lush roads. The spindly trees I remembered now overarched the walks. The day was not sunny, and the soft light was, I think, better for a rehearsal of the past. There were no glaring contrasts, only blendings of greenery against the library arches.

Shirley dropped me at the entrance to my building. The lettering on the doors was so preciously vivid; even the "Pull" was clear, shining like a gem as I walked into the building alone. The downstairs hall was waxed and gleaming as I maneuvered easily around students and strangers. The elevator surrounded me with walls of polished panels.

In the history office I first saw Clare's smiling black face, then Connie with her high blond hair. We all hugged, but I could not talk much, my voice breaking. The center table in the mail room looked small compared to when I skirted it by feel alone. I saw the coffeemaker and looked forward to pouring my own boiling water for tea, instead of waiting for someone to help, as I did when afraid of burning.

Oliver Johnson, whom I had known for over thirty years, was outside in the hall. I noticed the lines in his face but said nothing about them. He went with me into my office for the first time, like Gabriel at the pearly gates. The soft and sepia colors of my Indian *posters and the Navajo rug on the wall drifted back through years of remembrance. Little things surprised me. The paperback edition of Royce's* California *(which I knew so well through readers) was on the corner of my desk, and I saw the cover's bold drawing of John Charles Frémont. No one had told me that the publisher used Frémont for the cover. The printer to my talking computer was strangely white instead of my imagined black. The disk drive was about twice the size I had thought.*

In these first weeks, physical dimensions and proportions, not just colors and patterns, amazed me time after time. I have already noted the breadth of highways; here the confusions came in the mail room table and the disk drive. Familiar rooms surprised me as longer or shorter or wider. Doors were much too low; their width was predictable, but their height almost made me duck. While blind, proportions without utility had been forgotten, like the height of the door in contrast with its width.

These confusions of size and dimension are common in psychological studies of regained sight. The blind consciousness of space is very different from the visual. Its base is the reach of an arm or the length of a white stick. On recovering vision, the forms of objects are integrated into the whole visual field. Their relationships do not come spontaneously but only after being observed many times. We do not learn a new language overnight.

The reader for the California history course, Donn Headley, dressed as I seldom saw him afterward in neat jacket and tie, walked with me to the class in Sproul 1102. Outside the elevator I caught myself before taking his arm in the habitual way, then relished the independence of walking straight through the middle of an open door. I carried my white cane with its swirled blue, something of an affectation, I suppose, but somehow I felt that I might need it. Confidence is not an automatic attribute, but this was the last time I used the white cane in any form. Along the walk I felt the exhilaration of choosing my own path through oncoming people.

When I entered the lecture room, the class of about fifty fell silent. I could see all their faces in front of me, tiered row upon row. The lights glowed. It took me a while to start, and then I could only say, "You'll never know how beautiful you are." I couldn't bring myself to explain anything more. With a kind of relief I jumped into the lecture. Luckily it was introductory material with no complicated slide show, no demands for careful attention.

I walked back to my office with Harry Lawton (he had grown so much rounder!). We jabbered away, but I must confess that my mind was really on the faces and forms of the thronging students through which we were passing: "many a rose-lipped maiden; many a light-foot lad." When Harry turned off, I walked on, magnificently alone.

In our fourth-floor hall, a man stood in my way and with smiling gestures made me understand that I was to guess who he was. I judged he was faculty, but there are probably twelve or fourteen new colleagues whom I know well but have never seen. Now I was being tested. He made not a sound, and I tried a few names but completely failed. Only when he laughed did I realize it was Mark Smith, our medievalist. I had never thought he was so rugged and muscular. Later I recognized Arch Getty without trouble, though his beard surprised me, as did Ken Barkin's.

Sharon was good-looking with unexpectedly dark hair. John made me think of a young British rock star. Ron moved busily through the halls. Roger seemed younger and shorter. June was petite and pretty. My *reader, Elizabeth, had long black hair and sparkling eyes.*

Biggest surprises of the day: the white dust of my beard when I open the electric shaver; the folds of material as a body moves in a shirt or dress; the delight in drinking from a water cooler without getting the stream all over my face; the wall of family pictures at home; one tall palm against a white cloud in a deep blue sky. Tonight I paraphrased Shakespeare:

From years of gray, the world almost disguising,
Happily I see the sky, and then my state,
Like to the lark at break of day arising
From sullen dark, sings hymns at light's bright gate.

WEDNESDAY AND THURSDAY, APRIL 2–3. *Reported this morning for the first meeting of my Western America graduate seminar for the spring term. There are ten students. Many of their names I was familiar with, but now I saw their faces, their wild hairdos, their T-shirts with messages. (One had a big "C" on it; I thought of my first confrontation with the eye chart.) It did not take long to feel how much easier to remember names and carry on a discussion when faces and movements are apparent. I used my previously prepared braille notes. There had been no time to transcribe. But I made new notes beside the braille with ballpoint pen.*

My relationships with students would soon change. As hard as I worked during the blind time to maintain my share of graduate students, it became painfully clear that for dissertation advisers, the students were choosing other faculty when they might logically have come to me. Some of this was a subtle consequence of counseling in the department. Colleagues never said it, but they must have reckoned that the careful criticism of a doctoral dissertation is difficult enough with sight and without sight is virtually impossible. Students probably assumed the same, fearing their precious work might end as a poorly spelled, grammatically shaky, weakly criticized opus. I cannot prove that faculty and students considered me a danger in that way; maybe they weren't even fully aware of it themselves, but I do know that the number of my doctoral students fell dramatically during the blind years.

I came home with Irwin and Sarah Wall. His face is more angular than I remembered, and he has no beard now. She seemed lovely to me. The walk to the parking lot was beautiful—the landscaping now manicured into green vistas. What a change from those wild fields I remember. At home the Walls came in for a glass of sherry. Irwin had driven me home hundreds of times in the last fifteen years and on winter nights often stopped for sherry by the fire. We wondered if those times were about to end.

The Thursday morning lecture went well. This time I digressed to tell them about my eye surgery, what I could not bring myself to say on Tuesday. They were very quiet.

During the lecture we saw the short film Ishi. *[For years I had used that film in California history courses to suggest the human dimension of California Indian dispossession.] The countless times I have heard it all vanished. It was like a completely new experience to watch again those placid scenes of Indian patience with chipping stones or tanning hides and the leathered face of Ishi himself, compassionate, bewildered.*

Curious that I walked from Ishi *to a meeting between the history department and two very much alive California Indians, Rupert and Jeannette Costo. The Costos were discussing their endowment for a chair in Indian history, and the session had already begun. How I used to dread being late to meetings, tapping around with my stick, feeling my arm helplessly pulled toward an empty chair. Now I easily found a place and didn't disrupt anything.*

This was an unusual event, though, because I was

seeing many members of the department for the first time. The meeting droned on while my eyes searched the circle of faces, one after the other. About half I had seen in the last few days, but the others not yet. There was Carlos Cortés. There was Sarah Stage, whom I felt I knew so well; I saw her round, warm face, immediately appealing. Ed Gaustad's kindly chiseled face swam up through the mists of time. I suppose I can be excused for not paying much attention to the discussion.

Tonight at home Shirley and I lit the fireplace and I watched in fascination all those nervous, blue and orange tongues as if I had never seen them before. The sound of the fire used to be soothing, but the color and movement easily double the pleasure.

In the shower, I feel like an adolescent discovering my body. I am happily surprised that the proportions are not as bad as I had imagined. My vision still does strange things. I would like to think that the veins and ridges and shiny knuckles on my aging hands are not as obvious as they appear to me now. The hair on my arms and body is not distinct, but looks more like darker splotches. I do not understand why some things seem so sharp to me and others so blurred. I knew the hair on my head had receded, but my forehead looks terribly extended. In the merciless cross light of the

bathroom mirror, I see a mass of wrinkles with the
slightest facial movement.

There is much of vanity in this return to observation of one's body. Vanity is closely related to sight. I already part my hair more carefully. What must it have looked like through all those years of finger-felt parting? I want my body to look better, to be more muscular, to lose fat on that stomach. I rationalize I must do so for Shirley's sake, but I know there is ego there and self-esteem. Like our faces, our bodies are the locus of our selves. A sharpened image of our body means a fuller image of our self. Since the blind do not have that image, is it easier for them to rely on the spiritual dimension of self? It is "a grace bestowed on the blind," said Karl Bjarnhof, to have "an eye for the unseen." It was not Little Big Man but the blind shaman who was psychic and otherworldly. Must the sighted, especially the newly sighted, work harder to emphasize the spiritual?

The body, too, is the locus of sex. Here the analogy I made earlier between new sight and adolescence comes to mind. I have moved from the simple innocence of blindness into adolescent egotism and temptations. Now I admit to an obsession with sex. It's a good thing I'm married and Shirley is willing. We read together Alex Comfort's *Joy of Sex* and then *More Joy of Sex*, and I love it all. There is so much of visual pleasure in viewing the human body, so much of visual excitement in the act of sex. I know well that the blind can compensate, can internalize, can imagine and fantasize, and at the supreme moment of intercourse there is nothing that sight can add. The primary sense in sex is touch, not sight, but sight does reinforce direct intimacy. It is not easy to separate sexual longing from the visual image of the one who might satisfy it. Hull admitted that, too. Perfumes and soft voices are pretty insubstantial compared to what one sees of a woman.

Thus I found myself with an excessive interest in the human body, whatever that might mean for sex itself. The blind are imprisoned in their bodies; the body is for them almost synonymous with their environment. Consciousness is of the body walking, not of the hills and trees toward which they move. Now I see my own body from outside as well as from within. I see it sagging with age, not just feel its creaking. I can compare it with others and dream of my body being as vibrant as those I see. These are not just liberations; they are expansions of myself and my whole environment, intensely enlarging consciousness of self and others.

FRIDAY, APRIL 4. *Shirley left me alone in the waiting room at Kaiser. I was able to find the men's room by myself, and I was almost proud to walk directly to the urinal. Gone are the dismal times of trying to find the facilities, knocking around with my cane till I found the desired shape, feeling for the handle above, and then hoping for the right aim.*

Dr. Killeen was happy. The pressure was 12, way down. She noticed a small iritis activity, but thought it to be expected following surgery. Perhaps, though, it explains the few, early-morning pains. I asked about the rays of crystal shards that cross the eye when a bright light strikes it at night. She explained the cause as part of the surgery. The long uveitis and iritis had left the iris stubbornly rigid and undilatable. In order to remove the cataract through such an opening, a tear would likely occur, leaving an uneven aperture. To avoid that, she trimmed small notches at various points around the iris. Light refracts from the anchor points on the lens through these cuts. The problem, if it can be so called, will minimize in time. But at night I will always see halos around lights. And my iris will never open and close normally.

The excitement of this visit came when Dr. Killeen held out some tentative optimism about reading, at least normal-sized print. The intraocular lens is primarily for distance. If reading comes, it will not be for four to six weeks. Then she will prescribe glasses. You might imagine how happy that prospect looms! Direct study again—books, magazines, documents. Holding a volume of poetry and reading to Shirley once more. Seeing that computer screen and writing on it, revising my own words. Researching at the Huntington Library, working all on my own again. Maybe!

Every so often I get a kind of sinking feeling that there is a hidden negative here. I have thought enough about my work in the past to wonder how much I have been given the benefit of the doubt, special consideration because I was blind. If there has been such a double standard and if it explains some of my accomplishments, how hard will it be to have sight pull out the prop? When blind I was distinctive, out of the ordinary. Now I will be just like everybody else.

SATURDAY, APRIL 5. Harris Department Store today. Great fun to look at a hundred flamboyant tie patterns and pick out a paisley, bright blue and red. In the next case was a pair of green socks, the finest Kelly green you've ever seen. I thought of Sylvia but decided I wasn't quite yet ready for them. Instead I helped Shirley choose some jewelry. I think she liked my being

there. Neither of us needed what we bought, but nei-
ther did we care.

Vision improves almost every day. When I get out of
bed, I look first at the Yale prints to see how many more
towers I can pick out or whether I can count the pillars
of the Center Church on the Green. Then I test the pat-
tern on the Oriental rug—new circles emerge within
larger circles and darker details materialize as if by
magic. At breakfast I find myself using the English
etchings across the living room as vision charts, each
day seeing the arches more clearly on Lavenham
church or the Ely cathedral.

About ten years ago we bought a small condominium on the coast north of San Diego in the village of
Carlsbad, a couple of hours drive from home. We used
it as an escape from Riverside. It stood on a hill behind
the town, and from our windows the sea stretched wide
below. The joys of that place were indescribable, especially for a blind man, walking on the beach on an
early summer morning or a windy winter day, with
only the touch of Shirley's hand for guidance, gulping
in the sea air to the sounds of waves and seagulls. It
should not be hard to imagine how anxious I was to see
it now.

FRIDAY, APRIL 11. *Today we made our first foray to Carlsbad. Highway 15 seemed as broad as all outdoors and the pastures in the Temecula area greener than green. Down the final hill and there above Carlsbad were the commercial flower fields in full bloom— pinks and yellows and reds and lavenders—ranunculi laid in wide bands across the slopes. It was like filling my retina with reservoirs of color, compensating for the past in one gluttonous moment. When we got to our place, the ocean was covered by mist, but slowly the fog lifted and then I saw the sea, incredibly bright in that cerulean blue I dreamed of.*

Carlsbad was an unrecycled experience. I did not know that area at all before my blindness. In contrast, everything in Riverside was tinged with the early years of sight, and even new experiences were framed with old pictures, faint and dimming perhaps but still present. Our place in Carlsbad represented ten blind years, and the images there amassed were therefore the stuff of sound, though I should not say any less the stuff of substance.

Carlsbad, then, was like many a new place we had visited and loved during the blind years. As a matter of fact, driving along the highway, Shirley had asked me to name the places we need to revisit, like the Grand Tetons and Jenny Lake, where I have been but which I still must see.

Travel already takes on a new prospect. Looking back, I wonder whether trips were really worth the trouble. I know, even the blind collect new data, meet new people (i.e., hear new voices), and can tell a few new stories when they get back. But if the blind collect data, it has little to do with what their sighted peers collect. The vividness of nature and the convolutions of architecture are not easy to capture without sight. Every new hotel room is not taken in with the sweep of an eye but must await a painstaking tapping and groping. I agree with Hull that for the blind, travel leaves a lot to be desired. Until Russell discovered the tandem bicycle, he thought travel boring. "I never could get any sense of the country through which I was passing." Thurber, even before he went completely blind, had reservations about those "mistaken exits and entrances" and rather than ever travel again, "thought of spending the rest of my days wandering aimlessly around the South Seas, like a character out of Conrad, silent and inscrutable."

So in Carlsbad I began to feel rising in me an unexpected desire to see the world. Those tensions over travel were falling away. That Carlsbad sea and those hills of flowers were not just polishings of old experiences but new and intensely different, and they called for more.

Our condominium struck me as smaller but full of color with happy combinations of details, like Allison's childhood paintings (so like Joan Miró), the wood-framed mirror behind the couch, the printed bedsheets that Shirley had used for wall coverings. Dimensions and distances here puzzled me again. The buildings below our balcony were much closer than I had placed them, the garages more crowded together.

That night Dick and Pat arrived from Tucson, as planned. Somehow I thought my brother had grown much heavier during the fifteen years, but in fact he and Pat both looked trim. I noticed how agile Pat was and how little she has aged. It was a wonderful reunion. We had a champagne celebration with our good neighbor, Helen, and continued it the next evening at the Stoutenboroughs [they had moved to Carlsbad about the same time we got our place]. Phyllis wore a striking red dress and Don had pulled screaming red swim shorts over his white pants to test if I would notice. I did. Big laugh!

Over the years Don has been one of the few people close enough and honest enough to laugh with me over the punches, to have a good time when I mixed a brown with a black shoe. Others were often hesitant to mention such things. For me this kind of laughter from friends bridged the gap, made the whole matter more human, less coldly distant. It is good now to feel that laughter carrying on.

SATURDAY, APRIL 12. *Today we walked along the cliffs, watched for whales, and then went down to the beach and the water's edge. I had forgotten the pattern of foam among the breakers. The gliding of gulls close before us was sheer delight. We walked hand in hand, not because I needed to but because I wanted to.*

On the way back to Riverside, Shirley and I stopped for a brunch-celebration with some old friends, the Grispinos. A strange thing happened. Shirley took a snapshot of Charlotte and Joe standing before their fireplace over which was a large abstract print by Georgia O'Keeffe. In the center of the print was a field of bright blue, the same color I saw during surgery. When we had the snapshot developed, there in the middle of Georgia O'Keeffe's field of blue was my face, though I had not been in the picture. I had been standing behind the camera, and the flashbulb caught my reflection in precisely that spot, a weird coincidence.

MONDAY, APRIL 14. *Tonight we went to my first movie since the surgery. It was* Room with a View *and, no exaggeration, it assaulted me with the glory of my gift. I suppose that particular film may have done something similar to many sighted people as well, but to me it was rare beyond description. The intense close-ups of faces struck me most; had movie makers done that fifteen years before? What a gorgeous film— summery Italian hillsides, the backdrop of Florence, lush English gardens, a pretty Helena Bonham-Carter, even the fun of nude men at the swimming hole—a feast for a return to full-fledged moviedom.*

Trip to Bountiful came next, but no film ever approximated, probably none ever will, the delight of *Room with a View.*

The journal begins to become sporadic, not from jadedness but from bustle and distraction. Appointments with Dr. Killeen, however, brought me back to the record.

TUESDAY, APRIL 29. *Five weeks from surgery, I saw Dr. Killeen this morning. The vision tested at*

20/80, or slightly better, not much improvement over two weeks ago. But the examination was positive. She found no iritis or uveitis activity, thought the retina looked fine, and entered the pressure as 15. She told me the eye was now as strong as a normal eye, no longer needing protective glasses in daytime or shield at night. The Pred Forte drops may be reduced to one a day, though she would like that dose continued for a month or two as a precaution. I should be ready for glasses in ten days or two weeks; both distance and reading vision will thereby be improved. Because of the scars on the cornea, however, she recommends that I get separate glasses for each, not bifocals, having a complete lens for each kind of vision.

I asked if the cataract could ever return. The answer was no. Though with some cases a secondary dimming of vision can develop after surgery from the clouding of the surface behind the lens, in my case an incision was made to admit the light through that area, as mentioned earlier, and therefore the dimming problem could not develop. The cataract has indeed been conquered in the right eye. The only question there is how far the vision will go, whether reading and driving will ever be possible. And it's too early, she says, to discuss an operation on the other eye.

In the minor surgery room she trained her micro-scopes on the recuperating eye and removed three stitches from the fourteen. The removals would correct for astigmatism, and I should see the effects within forty-eight hours. Some relief may come with the dou-ble vision I have at night.

WEDNESDAY, APRIL 30. *This morning I was amazed at the improvement, largely, I assume, from the removal of those few stitches. I saw new patterns on the rug, cows and people in the Yale prints, and un-seen arches in the Lavenham church. I think if I were tested today the vision would be at least 20/70.*

8

Second Chance

Since the journal sputtered out in the face of routine, I must summarize the eventualities. What a year it was! My vision with glasses improved to 20/40, which, even with only one eye, met the minimal requirements for driving. The Department of Motor Vehicles gave me a two-year license, and I became a teenager with his first car. I learned the buttoned instructions of the automatic teller machine and marveled at how much the technology of money had escalated in fifteen years. Shirley and I read the newspaper over breakfast like old married couples do, and we talked about the news, interrupting each other's reading, as if nothing was ever different.

We took trips to Santa Cruz in both the summer and the fall. I should have noticed California more crowded, drearier, more polluted. Eventually disagreeable facts would penetrate, but in these first months it all seemed quite the contrary. On the way to Santa Cruz I was struck by the landscaping of freeways in towns and cities. From the car I saw again the line that sweeps along between the rows of grapevines and lettuce, embedded pattern in apparent chaos. The oaks still hugged the hills. I moved freely into motel rooms without having to feel them out with my cane. And, above all, I saw again my daughter, Allison, after fifteen years (half her lifetime). Her boys, Skye and Christopher, were now five and three years old. I read to them. I took them to the library. I watched their faces as they laughed and their mouths turn down when their mother cried.

Before the year was out I got a new computer and felt the trauma of dismantling my old ITS talking Hungarian. It was like putting a friend in a box and shipping him off. I took it down to the campus handicapped services as a gift to a blind student and felt a little dizzy when I came back.

In my working life, reluctant to face the freeways, I took the intercampus bus to the Huntington Library every week or so. The fifteen years had seen some dramatic additions to the Huntington, including a whole

new wing to the research area. I walked those magnif-
icent, carpeted halls beside the paintings and tapes-
tries. I pulled down reference books at leisure. I will
always remember the first day I sat in a plush armchair
and perused the scholarly journals, picking them up,
then laying them down at the whim of a title or a picture. Few places on earth see scholarship conducted in
so lovely a setting, and now it was open to me again,
doors wide. On the practical level, that year I finished
two articles, from start to finish, without braille!

As grateful as I had been to readers and braillewrit-
ers and talking computers, I knew that they were like
horses and buggies compared to the bullet train of the
scanning eye. The blind are subjected to what Potok
called "the slow and random ooze of information." A
reader usually painstakingly reports every detail. The
tape gives the book word for word, and skipping is
chancy. The active eye, however, can dart across the
page of an old newspaper and in a fraction catch relevant particulars while it skips the garbage.

That is the essence of reading, and I must shed at
least one tear here, not in pity but in regret, for the
blind who cannot have it. I save my pity for the sighted
who can but do not. I know why Clark, blind "bard and
scribbler," castigated the young.

"Oh," she said, "they can make out the words, but I mean read—Homer for instance, or history, or anything intelligent people for thousands of years have been willing to give an arm or a leg to have opened to them. (And I, what would I give to have it back again, for a week, for one day—?)."

I wish I could share it with you, Eleanor Clark, the chance to read and scan that was given back to me.

Several times this winter Dr. Killeen said that we probably should go ahead with removal of the cataract from the left eye. It was not an open and shut case. There were residual fears, at least in my mind, that the regained vision in the good right eye might be affected by surgery in the left. I knew it had happened with Thurber. The arrow that in a childhood accident blinded his one eye brought on a sympathetic ophthalmia in the other, a condition that eventually blinded that eye as well. Russell lost his second eye from sympathetic ophthalmia after the first was traumatized sightless by a flying iron splinter. Dr. Killeen, however, reassured me that although such carry-over from eye to eye occurred in earlier surgeries, it was much less frequent now. In the end she left it up to me to take the chance, but she made it clear that it will probably have to be done someday, when the mature cataract leaks as the right one had, and it is far better to preempt the emergency.

In February I wrote to Dr. Killeen that I was ready to go ahead with the second surgery. The date was set for April 16. On April 2, I was scheduled for an A-scan, an ultrasonic measurement for the lens implant. After two tries, the first technician called in a second who tried twice again. They said the discrepancies in the length of the eye (unusually short) were so great they would like the doctor to review the situation before they proceeded.

Dr. Killeen explained to me that the left eye had undergone phthisis, a frequent and dreaded outcome of surgery in eyes with uveitis. In my case, that damage had already occurred before surgery. The eye had shrunk to about 18 millimeters (a normal eye is 23–25 mm). There was some danger of corneal disintegration as a result of surgery, but she said if that happened, we could transplant a new cornea, and that would produce a more comfortable eye in any case. Once again, she remained optimistic.

On April 15, pre-op day, we began early with a B-scan of about ten pictures. I looked over the technician's shoulder as he pasted them on the chart and asked what those white blips were in some of the vitreous areas. He said, "Those are the things we wish weren't there." Shortly afterward, I saw Dr. Killeen again. "The eye," she said, "is so short—the result of the long uveitis—that no available lens will do the proper focusing. So we will use the largest, most powerful available. That will make a nearsighted eye at best, and we probably cannot expect any sharp images. But even seeing shapes without details, like cars coming from the left, will be useful." The pressure was 19 in each eye, well within normal.

I started the journal again in expectation, this time handwritten, not in braille.

APRIL 16. *Reported for surgery at noon. In the admitting room saw Inez Staubel, a jolly woman of 74 years whom I had joked with yesterday about her preference for the red lollipops in a jar on the anesthetist's desk. Now we discovered we were both to have a cataract removed by Dr. Killeen that afternoon. Together we kissed wife (mine) and children (hers) and at Dante's Gate marched with the nurses into the preparation room.*

Inez was terrified, shaking at the prospects of IV and blood pressure monitor, which recalled for her a previous nightmarish surgery. As we lay on our beds side by side, having our vital signs taken and being medicated, I could jabber on about my experience of a year ago, and it seemed to help her. She was born in Trinidad, had married a Swiss in this country, and was very proud of her seven children. The IV reduced her to tears, and I was glad she went first to surgery so that her period of terror was shortened.

For me the preparation smacked of old home week. Dolores, the IV injectionist, claimed to remember me. Of course, last year I only felt but never saw her. Dave, the anesthetist, having heard about "Mr. Sunshine," introduced me to the others as a celebrity. (How little we control the ways by which we are remembered!)

In the surgery I saw all the equipment, the craned microscopes, the blood pressure monitors, the masked faces bending over mine, which last year were only voices and echoes. Now with my good eye I could see Dr. Killeen. She was in drab green, not the white I had imagined last time. She looked into the pupil. She said it had not dilated much, so she would have to take care of that herself [a sector iridectomy]. The first would be the worst.

When she began cutting, it felt as if she were coming in around the outside of the eyeball. I winced, and that was the last I knew. The anesthetist blocked me out, *robbing me of my dancing lights in the electric-blue field and of ever knowing whether they were still there.*

Though I vaguely recall spilling two cups of soup in the recovery room, the first thing I really remember was waking in my own bed at nine that night. Shirley said I had talked with Dr. Killeen, helped dress myself, walked from wheelchair to car, undressed at home, done what she suggested like going to the bathroom, and gotten into bed. But I remember none of it.

GOOD FRIDAY, APRIL 17. *At eleven, Inez, two of her daughters with grandchildren, Shirley, and I were reunited in Dr. Killeen's waiting room. Pat, last year's vision in a space suit, took off my bandages. This time from the operated eye I could see very little—vague objects passing across pools of light, and those only in the bottom and left field of vision. There is no implanted lens there to help either. In the second operation, because of the phthisis, Dr. Killeen was unable to insert one. The lens she had implanted in the right eye was 13 diopters. The maximum made is 30, and the left eye required 43 diopters.*

She could not yet see into the retina since the cornea is still too swollen and inflamed. It is possible, however, that the retina has in places folded over itself as the result of the phthisis, blocking vision in certain areas. We will know more in a few weeks as the eye settles down.

She held out the hope of gaining some vision through eventual use of a powerful, soft contact lens, the kind prescribed for infants after removal of congenital cataracts. I noticed a black spot floating around in the lower vision. Dr. Killeen said it was an air bubble that will soon absorb.

Inez fared much better. When her bandages came off, she saw her children and grandchildren clearly, and I told her to expect much more in the weeks ahead. She was fearless enough now to sign up that very day for removal of her other cataract in June.

HOLY SATURDAY, APRIL 18. *The eye hurt in the night and is still highly inflamed this morning. But when cleaning off the lids, Shirley thought it looked somewhat less red, and at breakfast I might have seen a bit more than yesterday. It is still nothing but blobs of almost formless light mainly on the left edges.*

Disappointment! Letdown! Compare last year! Miracles raise unreasonable expectations. I was never promised more than I am getting, but the other eye turned out so much better than predicted that hope wormed in. I must close my good eye and think how Mary Burton would cherish even that clouded fuzz of a world! Open again, and I write this journal and follow the lines on the paper instead of the way I began it a year ago on a clanking braillewriter; I could drive myself to church tomorrow instead of being led there with a white cane—come on, friend, how much more do you want!

EASTER SUNDAY. *Service at St. George's was lovely. No one but Father Gene knew of my second operation, which was just as well. I did tell Mary Burton, though, and wished her a Happy Easter. She twisted her head as if in dialogue with herself and contradicting her comment of last year, said, "There's always hope."*

The eye is still very inflamed, but the twinges of pain don't come now more than once or twice an hour. Air bubble gone.

MONDAY, APRIL 20. *Eye quite painful last night, as if the salve (Dexasporin) bothered it. I wondered if the cut iris, trying to expand at night, would cause the pain. Much less pain in the daytime. Eye still red ("bloody" as Shirley says). But I do think I see more shapes than yesterday—wishful thinking? I find myself walking around with the good eye closed to catch gross patterns (white walls, pictures, bed, countertops).*

TUESDAY, APRIL 21. *Little if any pain last night. Phoned Pat, Dr. Killeen's nurse, to ask why eye still so* blood red. She said there had been hemorrhaging, which would absorb in time. No worry. Vision about the same.

WEDNESDAY, APRIL 22. *To campus and office this a.m. Vision may be better. On one side of the left field of vision I can tell fingers against a white wall.*

FRIDAY, APRIL 24. *Dr. Killeen was encouraging today; in fact, her lovely face was all smiles by the time we left. She found no uveitis, and she could see enough of the retina to know that it was all attached (though it was not yet clear enough to observe scarring). The nurse (Pat) recorded my vision as hand motion at three feet, and Dr. Killeen felt, considering that the cornea is still swollen, that we may get more vision than expected. She did not take the pressure for fear of disturbing the eye, but she expected it would be unusually low.*

As for the future, I asked if we could implant a lens later, and she said no. Lenses are just not made strong enough, and she would not want to subject that eye to any additional surgery. If a corneal transplant were ever necessary, there are some possibilities in that connection. She returned positively to the prospect in about eight weeks of a permanent infant contact lens to be worn with glasses.

I can wash hair again but shouldn't do exercises yet.

SATURDAY, APRIL 25. *My vision creates a divided world. On the left is the mist of Monet's haystacks or the fuzzy confusion of Jackson Pollock; on the right, the precision of a William Harnett or a Norman Rockwell. Walking down a hall with these two worlds moving close on either side is what I imagine a jumbled mind to be, or perhaps a bird's vision of two unfused images. There is still a middle section in the left vision which is much less clear than the outer edges. The outer parts now remind me of the very first day a year ago when the bandages came off.*

Tonight went to a party for Sharon Salinger given by John Phillips, Arch Getty, and Sarah Stage. When asked about the surgery, I played the role of optimist in the spirit of the drinks, but I wonder how much I convinced anyone.

SUNDAY, APRIL 26. *The eye was uncomfortable and didn't seem to improve much. My birthday was a quiet one, though there were family phone calls. We went to church, and the Graebners came down after dinner for Shirley's special lemon soufflé.*

MONDAY, MAY 11. *Dr. Killeen found the cornea healing very well, though there is still enough edema to block full details of the retina. Everything she could see, however, looked encouraging. Pressure in the right eye was 17. She will talk with the optometrist, and on June 1 the eye will be measured for the contact lens. I can swim now (but not get water in the eye), do exercises, and sleep on my left side. No more patch and salve at night, but the drops continue.*

I do not know how much was disappointment or discouragement, but I suspect these emotions were more responsible this time for the journal beginning to peter out. At this point, a month followed with no entries.

MONDAY, JULY 13. *In the morning the optometrist instructed me in the insertion and care of the new contact lens for the left eye.*

In the afternoon saw Dr. Killeen. She had to relocate the contact lens, which had drifted to the top of the eye. I frankly can't tell the difference whether or not the lens is in place. The operation, however, looked fine to her, the cornea healing nicely with no complications. The punctil plug she had put in the left tear duct a few weeks ago to keep the eye more moist she took out, thinking it might be causing some irritation. I am to change to daily drops of FML (Fluorometholone, a less powerful cortisone than Pred Forte).

The pressure in the right eye was 17, and in the vision tests, it continues to amaze us all. I actually got one or two of the letters on the 20/30 level, but it wasn't easy.

TUESDAY, JULY 14. *The optometrist looked at the contact lens again after a night of use. He tested the vision and proclaimed the left eye to have 20/750, which he estimates to be about twice as good as before the contact lens. He wants me to wash the eye with a saline solution morning and night because of the extra mucus and to come in for cleaning instructions in two weeks. In two months he will consider new glasses to bring the good right eye up to its potential.*

The journal ends there. That spring of 1987 emphasized the sad fact that cataract operations do not invariably succeed. The contact lens made so little practical difference that in a few weeks I abandoned it as not worth the trouble. Rapunzel's tears do not always bring sight to the prince. Johann Sebastian Bach was operated on twice for cataracts. David Blackhall underwent four unsuccessful operations for cataracts before going totally blind. Thurber, too, suffered four abortive surgeries before he gave up in blindness. My success rate, one out of two, was at least better than that.

So I would remain one-eyed. I could hear Mr. Squiers in *Nicolas Nickleby* saying of me, "He has but one eye, and the popular prejudice runs in favour of two." The fact left me with no depth perception, but that did not trouble me much since I came to it from the path of blindness. Had I lost one eye while seeing with both, the problem of depth perception would have loomed large.

Sometimes the idea of one eye bothered me. Somewhere I read of a primitive culture where the one-eyed are feared as the children of the devil. Such abnormalities suggested an evil eye, which could at will dispense death and destruction. In that society, I remember reading, children who have sight in one eye were occasionally blinded by their parents, for the life of the blind was preferable to living with an eye that might be an evil eye. I have tried in vain to confirm such a society. It is a disturbing story with frightening implications, but I console myself that, even if it is true, everything cultural is relative. In his Danish school for the blind, Bjarnhof suffered his faint peripheral vision as an "unnatural vice." The Cyclopes with one eye were monsters, but so was Argus, and he had one hundred eyes. "In the country of the blind, the one-eyed man is king."

I began noticing in history the figures with one eye. Tamerlane led his Mongolian hordes. Hannibal crossed the Alps to ravage Italy. At Copenhagen, Lord Nelson avoided a distasteful order by putting his blind eye to the glass; at Trafalgar, he even commanded his *Victory* with one eye. Big Bill Haywood fought like a tiger for his Western miners. The modern Moishe Dayan indeed glamorized the eye patch as he organized the military defense of his Israel. Those one-eyed seemed a pretty violent crew, but then there was Sammy Davis, Jr., who only quipped about his disability. In a golf tournament he was once asked what his handicap was, and he answered, "I'm a colored, one-eyed Jew."

As with Sammy Davis, it mattered little that I could use but one eye now—except for a fundamental feeling, the fear of losing my sight again, more fearsome when there is only one eye to lose.

Far more interesting was the continuing unfolding of the implications of second sight. I noticed changes as I spoke with students. Talking with troubled undergraduates is a challenge for anyone. Their immediate difficulties with classes, papers, and exams sometimes spill over into more personal problems—parents, girlfriends, finances, deaths, fears, and insecurities. And then the Kleenex box must be dredged out of the top drawer. In these situations I could now predict the tears by visual means—the pursed or bitten lips, the downcast eyes, the moist eyelids. How many of those revelations had I missed when blind? The sounds—pauses, cleared throats, sighs, breathing, the voice—always gave some clues. But plenty of others were missed without the total impact of a face. All the hints are there now. I am in control. The Kleenex comes on time.

I see people smile. I wonder if I do not smile myself more often. Friends tell me I look happier, more confident, and that could be the reason. I can smile back. A blind smile, Hull says, is like sending off a dead letter. Now my letters are answered. When Hocken got her sight back, her friends told her she looked "more alive. . . . You're using expression." She herself felt facial muscles she had never used before.

I walk straighter. In the period following the first surgery, when I passed department store mirrors, I noticed that I bent as I walked. I must have fallen into that habit as I held my two arms forward like a wedge to avoid half-open doors. The Seeing Eye people hope to get their blind subjects early for training with dogs before bad habits of posture and gait are ingrained. It's an ego boost to see myself in front of a mirror more erect with my stomach pulled in.

A hard habit to break is counting steps. This comes so naturally for the blind that it goes without saying. It's just plain efficient to know how many steps from the door of the garage to the gate, from the office to the men's room, and it means survival to know how many steps to the descending stairs. But I still do it, and when my mind is not otherwise occupied, I find myself counting steps wherever I go.

Names were vitally important to me when blind. If a conversant was not gracious enough to tell me his or her name and I was not clever enough to identify the voice, I got so I would simply ask. I needed to know that name. It was a raft in a slippery sea. If I already knew the person, the name filled in the past; if I did not, it was the base to build on. Now I am much more at ease talking with someone whose name I cannot remember or do not know. I realize the name will come in its own time, and I can relax while the visual clues pile up.

The sight of another person is a reinforcement of the self. We know what we are because we can compare ourselves with others. However much we cannot do that, our own selves become that much less distinct. In his blindness, Hull often feels like "a mere spirit, a ghost, a memory" because others have become "disembodied voices, speaking out of nowhere, going into nowhere."

Is it possible that some of my interest in my own body, my own sexuality, is related to a more distinct self? That seems far-fetched to me, but it is true that I return to former roles I could not play when blind. As with all the crippled, paralyzed, or handicapped, the primary role of the disabled is disability, and that takes precedence over father, husband, breadwinner, or student. For me now, little things make these supporting parts emerge as leads again—driving myself to work, putting gas in the car, cleaning the garage, paying and tipping the waitress. My calling as disabled has been superseded by other roles, and I feel myself a more traditional person.

After spinal surgery Murphy felt that renewal: "I had been born again . . . in body and soul." Though I had established an equilibrium in blindness, now I felt a better balance, a more intended distribution of the senses, like an engine with all its cylinders running or a tree with evenly spread branches.

I wonder if my masculine role is reinforced. Looking back on the blind years, always walking a few feet behind my wife, holding her arm to lead me, being driven everywhere, letting her pay the check in restaurants, having nothing to do with the care and upkeep of the car, it was easy to magnify these as compromises of my masculine position. In gender clichés, the blind are no more liberated than any other group. It worried me that sightlessness was also blinding me to Shirley's needs. Did she ever crave a man who was more protective, who could recognize danger a mile away, who could instantly rise to stand between her and harm? I am no Arnold Schwarzenegger, no John Wayne, but I rally to the stereotypes with my sight restored.

Freud picked up on this connection. He coupled sight with sexual gratification and therefore could describe its loss in terms of castration. In a similar way there are vague implications in Aeschylus that Oedipus is blinded in retribution for his sexual transgressions. When Lear was toppled from his manly power as king, it seemed appropriate to Shakespeare to leave him blind. I suppose I reflected some of that instinctual stereotype myself when that short flash of a castration sense came over me during surgery. Does my feeling of the new roles I play support such literary insights? Only if we realize that we are dealing with symbols and social stereotypes. The blind are certainly not castrated. Their sexual gratification and masculine roles may be different in kind, but that can be said of many others.

Oliver Sacks tells of one of his neurological patients whose sense of smell suddenly intensified to unimaginable proportions. As a result he experienced a whole new aesthetic, which in his case was manifested by a disturbing inability to categorize objects that he saw. The immediacy of the particulars that he smelled overwhelmed his competence in making sense of those details. Heightened awareness got in the way of understanding. Some such intensified perception swept over me in this first year. I was not in the extreme disability of Sacks's patient, but it took months to be sure that I was seeing things as they really were. An experience, which once I had to internalize because it could not be seen in its wider environment, could now be externalized, expressed as seen and reciprocated back and forth between friends, loved ones, human beings. This sharpened comprehension of an enormous external environment combined with a different sense of my own internal self must surely be the fundamental inheritance of my second sight.

I have not lost my devotion to order. That was either encoded in me at birth or developed so early that in practice it amounts to the same thing. Order made blindness acceptable and manageable. I could find what I needed and go on from there. Now that same order explodes outward, and I see it far beyond my own control. Diderot in the eighteenth century thought that the sighted have an easier time proving the existence of God because they can more readily see the vast order created by his deistic Deity. Back we are with that other stereotype of the poor, unfortunate blind, in this case not even able to discern their God. Yet somehow I feel, do not ask me how, that my restored sight has brought me closer to the music of the spheres.

And all of this came with one eye. I shall never begrudge the second.

9

Renounce Your Ways of Seeing

Renounce your wicked, sinful ways of seeing. Admit that the sky above is solid and that your tales of moon and stars are but delusions. Accept the science and the philosophy of the blind, and we will not crucify you.

Those were powerful ideas to me when I read them in "The Country of the Blind," H. G. Wells's allegory of prejudice and intolerance. The blind spoke that way to Nunez, a sighted traveler who "in the wildest wastes of Ecuador's Andes" fell down a precipice into their isolated land. There from time immemorial all people had been congenitally blind, "generation after generation. They forgot many things; they devised many things." They lived in neat houses without windows and walked streets with notched guiding curbs. They worked in the cool night and slept in the warm day because light was irrelevant. Coming into this Shangri-la and remembering the old saying, Nunez expected to become king in the country of the blind. Over and over, however, his stumbling efforts in their dark world were thwarted by entrenched ways, including his own un-willingness to strike a blind person. After his one ex-plosion into violence, he was starved into submission and finally was reduced to a pitiful servant.

He fell in love with a beautiful maiden, but her fam-ily and the authorities judged him unacceptable for marriage. The scientists decided that the world he de-scribed to them, the sighted world, could only be the result of mental delusions revolving around his sight. If he were to have his eyes surgically removed, he might hope to become normal like them. The girl pleaded with him to do so, and desperately in love, he was ready to make the sacrifice. Before the sacrificial day, however, he walked to a quiet place and "saw the morning, the morning like an angel in golden armour, marching down the steeps. It seemed to him that be-fore this splendour he, and the blind world in the val-ley, and his love, and all, were no more than a pit of sin." Nunez looked on the trees and the mountains and, turning his back, began the slow bruising climb out of the valley of the blind "in which he had thought to be King."

I took Wells's allegory of intolerance and made it an allegory of misunderstanding between the worlds of the sighted and the blind. I became Nunez climbing out of the valley in which I had once thought to be a blind king. In that valley my early sighted years gave me an advantage that I was willing to capitalize on. Now I was again trying to be some kind of king, or maybe a prophet, because I had experienced both conditions.

Wells reinforced my sense that disability becomes a mortgage on one's thinking. That is the phrase that Murphy uses. Hull finds a different analogy—a vast vacuum cleaner sucking out past memories, interests, and perceptions of time and place and requiring their reconstruction. And I was learning, too, that second sight is the same, another reconstruction, a renascence, sucking out the reconstructions, inflating the once deflated into life again.

Nothing illustrates that pattern as much as the constructing and reconstructing of faces. I look back now and see faces as the unifying theme of my journal. I was overhauling the blind images of all those people around me, known and new, which had been sustained or created through the human voice. With a few close individuals, a very few, there had been some tactile contact. But though I was invited to do so on occasion,

I never much enjoyed feeling other people's faces. I felt like Wagner: "I'm scared I'll knock off a false eyelash or stick my finger up a nose. It's just not something I really want to do." The faces I knew were voices.

In the normal world touch and sound have different statuses in the hierarchy of the senses. For me when blind, they, of course, became commandingly important, but at the same time they often seemed only other gropings for the seen. A voice, for example, was a way to get at the shape of a head, the color of skin, the wrinkles of age. I can remember even listening intently to my own voice (and not liking it much); maybe it would help me know the changes in my own face.

When sight was restored, voices were suddenly reduced to a minor status, and I realized how misleading a source they can be. The sensations of a more complete personality, the color of skin and hair, proportions, gestures, and body language, left the old voice image radically transformed. The grays were suddenly swept out of the colors. The traditional hierarchy of the senses was reestablished but now with an understanding that the orthodox way was not unique and not necessarily superior.

Like Nunez, I was coming to understand that the blind—like all of us—are not alone. The blind react to a society that reacts to them. And it is not easy to assess the conflicting feelings that society holds. For one thing, the blind receive unusual consideration and attention. Why does Roget's *Thesaurus* list two-and-a-third columns of synonyms for blindness or dimsightedness but only half a column for deafness? Why does it give nearly twice as many synonyms for vision as for hearing? Why for generations have the blind been the only disabled to receive an additional exemption on their income tax? They are the "darlings" of the handicapped.

With some justification, of course. The eye is certainly the most remarkable seat of the senses. It encompasses the distant and the immediate; it is the most maneuverable; it swivels and turns; it closes off completely simply by shutting its lids; it changes and blurs as we squint; it includes clever protective mechanisms of tearing and blinking. To lose it is to lose a truly extraordinary instrument.

Surely this explains the deep and universal fear of blindness. "There but for the grace of God go I," and there is what I want least to be. Unfortunately, that tragic spirit, what Kenneth Jernigan calls "the disaster concept," often begets sentimentality; witness a bit from one syrupy book:

So sad is the fate of the blind, so mournful their doom, that all kind natures are eager to aid their helplessness, while even the harshest will stand aside in hushed reverence to let them grope their way along.

I know people who couldn't give me the time of day while I was sighted, but once I was blind, couldn't do enough for me. Feeling what the disabled Andre Dubus calls the universality of a wounded person, they magnify every little ordinary act of the blind into a deed of courage. When I washed dishes after meals, because it was easy and a simple contribution, I kept getting praised as if I were a saint. One friend delighted in saying that I scrubbed the tea kettle far beyond the point where her eyes told her it was clean; my "incredible" fingers still found shards of deposit on the bottom. Undoubtedly true, and believe me, I bear no resentment toward these good men and women, most of whom I cherish. They only exaggerate the feelings of the blind Congregationalist minister of Western Springs, Illinois: "Bob Kemper is like an elephant doing the ballet: It may not be a good ballet, but it is amazing he can do it at all."

Unfortunately I am aware of but have seldom felt a reverse reaction. The blind radio writer, Hector Chevigny, tells of a friend who confessed that he did not visit Chevigny in the hospital "for the same reason that [he] couldn't go to his funeral. [He] can't stand funerals." Yates describes such people as too "full of their own fitness" to face disability. I suspect that, in Orozco's Prometheus mural, they are the ones who shrink from the fire in contrast to those who reach out.

Another group in the society adds to the fear and the sentimentality a measure of antipathy. I have heard that it is good luck to touch the crippled, but I have never heard it good luck to touch the blind. Susan Sontag believes the reason cancer patients are lied to is "not just because the disease is (or is thought to be) a death sentence, but because it is felt to be obscene—in the original meaning of that word: ill-omened, abominable, repugnant to the senses." Something like that happens in attitudes toward the blind.

Perhaps the feeling is more accurately resentment, and it works in two directions, from both the sighted and the blind. The sighted can subconsciously see the blind as holding power—power to make others feel guilty or incompetent or awkward, the power of attracting attention. Their strengths can be envied. How easy it would be to yearn for Lusseyran's flashes of light; if for nothing else, they were pragmatically and vitally instrumental to the French Resistance.

Envy of such power is understandable and disturbing. The sighted may express this worry by an unwillingness to confront the blind, instead of asking the companion, as I heard many times, "Does he take sugar?" "Where would he like his cup?" Children reveal some of society's frustrations toward the blind. The stories of struck and taunted blind children, like Krentz and Russell and my friend Judith, are too numerous to ignore. Prejudice, said Chevigny, is basically prejudgment, and just as with a Negro or a Jew, the blind feel plenty of that.

We live in a culture in which young, perfect bodies are practically worshiped and supple physical activity is an end in itself, an attitude to which my new sight has made me highly vulnerable. Though everyone knows it is morally wrong to elevate strength and might over weakness, it hurts to look on the reverse. Disability bears thorny witness to the frailty of our existence, to the lurking threats to our ideas. Murphy puts it this way, throwing the emphasis on the sighted:

The disabled serve as constant, visible reminders to the able-bodied that the society they live in is shot through with inequality and suffering, that they live in a counterfeit paradise, that they too are vulnerable. We represent a fearsome possibility.

And Freud may be right that we symbolize that "fearsome possibility" by associating blindness with emasculation. That worship of perfect bodies is indeed a complicated emotion, and amid all of these fears and worries it must smolder beneath the facade of solicitous concern for the blind.

I know that the antipathy can also flow from the blind themselves. I understand the resentment that Hull feels when someone makes grandstand asides for his benefit. One lecturer, for example, with perfectly good intentions explained aloud and pointedly, "John, you may like to know that this color is yellow." By that remark Hull was excluded, segregated, subtly degraded. Chevigny went so far as to find in such acts a measure of aggressiveness, seeing in society's attitudes and stereotypes a prejudice that the blind are called on to fight. As he said,

Salvation for one who loses sight consists of avoidance of a vicious circle in which the world's fixed notion of the helplessness of the blind creates that helplessness, and their consequent exhibition of helplessness confirms the world in its fixed notion.

And the cycle comes full circle, because the sighted in putting down the blind ("Isn't it too bad that you can't see this as I do") might well exhibit an instinctual fear that the blind might have their own ways of seeing that could be highly effective, perhaps superior. It is rather like white people who have no desire to be black but still imagine, envy, fear, and resent black sexual vigor.

Superiority is resented, and embedded in the myths of the race are notions that the blind are superior. This hit me hardest when my friend Bill Brandon directed me to Ovid's story of Tiresias. Here was a young Theban walking in the woods and surprising two snakes mating. He had stumbled over the male and female wrestling in coitus over the secret of life. He struck them with his stick and was immediately altered into a woman. For seven years he lived completely female. Then, walking in the woods, he once more came across serpents coupling. He battered them again and was restored to the gender of his birth. Thereafter he lived as one who had known life as both male and female, one who was blessed with the heavenly ability to see the other person's point of view.

The scene shifts to Olympus where Zeus and Hera are feuding over the momentous issue of which sex has the greater pleasure in lovemaking (Zeus saying the woman; Hera, the man). In desperation they summoned Tiresias, graced with the gift to see both sides, to settle their argument. He sided with Zeus.

If the parts of love-pleasure be counted as ten,
Thrice three go to women, one only to men.

Hera, furious with the verdict, struck Tiresias blind. Unable to counter his wife's curse but pitying the begetter of his victory, Zeus endowed Tiresias with prophecy. So the blind prophet strode through Greek mythology as the wise man to whom heroes, including the great Odysseus, repaired for guidance.

Now, it should be clear that when blind, I never felt superior to anyone, believe me. I certainly did not see me of the gray socks as blessed with any special insights on sex. Yet the story caused me to wonder if I might not be in an unusual position to say something about blindness and sight. Though I never felt prophetic, I am willing to acknowledge that blind men like Lusseyran and Hull have used their blindness in ways that suggest modern Tiresiases. And it is sobering to remember that both of them contend that all blind people could have these gifts did not society relentlessly teach that the blind cannot see.

But I never saw copulating snakes, even in my dreams, and since I was one of those who were beau-

tifully protected in my blindness, I was largely immu-
nized from its mystical implications. But I did see a
connection between blindness and prophecy, and it
came in the uses of order. The future is best known by
those who prepare for it, and those who have order in
their soul are best prepared. Order is neither ordained
nor exclusive with the blind, but since ordering one's
life and work is so much more important when blind,
like a secondary sense it becomes emphasized. Perhaps it was only the sharpening of that logic of order
that Zeus bestowed on Tiresias.

If the blind are so susceptible to order and since order is fundamental to beauty (proportion, balance,
grace), then one would expect that the blind have a
special appreciation of the beautiful. But my limited
experience does not point that way. Sight seems so
much more helpful. In the first place, as I learned with
proportions and distances, sight makes it easier to
know and appreciate the nonutilitarian, and at least in
the extent to which beauty is nonutilitarian, sight becomes an instrument of beauty. True, in the blind years
I certainly experienced beauty—in music, in bird
songs, in the wind, in holding lovely shapes and forms.
Now, however, to the sound of the wind is added the
movement of tall grasses and white clouds; to music,

the instrument; to the bird song, the bird. How often in blindness the imagination simply translated the emotions of sound or touch into color or form or movement. Then vision was demanding its due. Sight must hold a priority among the senses in the realm of the beautiful.

I did learn, however, that vision may not be trustworthy, for during my first weeks of sight, it was hard to find anything, even our jumbled garage, that was not beautiful. I was the child again, fresh to the moment, unencumbered by layers of stale and stultifying responses. Oil-soaked rags revealed startling forms of color and pattern. It took weeks for reactions of shabbiness or gaudiness to impinge on the once wondrous things. If mature and critical artistic judgment requires vision, it also needs history, the dimensions of time and experience.

Sight, of course, is not advantageous only to beauty; it is a tool of efficiency. I am impressed over and over at how much easier and more direct are my sighted efforts. I sweep now only that part of the walk that has leaves on it, not the whole walk. I move straight through a door, not pausing to feel for the edges. My hand reaches faster for the cup on the shelf, and it places the plug in the socket without fear and fum-

bling. Longhand multiplication no longer involves remembering all the figures in my head. The toothpaste
goes directly onto the toothbrush (no longer on my
tongue for measurement). The electric shaver stops
clean-cut at the bottom of my sideburns. Most everything takes only half the time.

Do I miss the blind days? Admittedly, there are advantages for the blind. Concentration is easier without
sight, that I know. "A blind man benefits by lack of dis-
tractions" were Thurber's words, but he, unlike me,
was blessed with something approaching total recall,
and when he was almost completely blind, he could re-
peatedly pull fresh materials out of his past for stories
and especially for those pointed one-line cartoons. Totally blind and writing for the *New Yorker*, he was a
better, more productive writer than when he could see.
As he wrote, concentrating more and more on his remarkable memory, he rearranged his words over and
over "in that inner world of the blind and in the silence
of the night."

With new sight, that inner world is harder for me to
find, and my attention is frequently interrupted by the
diversions of the background. I find that arguments
during a meeting are more difficult to follow as my eyes
work their way over the scene—the books behind the

speaker, papers or dust jackets on the intervening table, the shining coffee jug and the inscribed mugs. Ac-
ademics spend a lot of time listening to one another
lecture. When blind I had little trouble catching the
steps in a colleague's argument; now the window over
the same speaker's shoulder frames a billowing euca-
lyptus, and my eyes are so anxious to enjoy it that my
mind loses another point in the development. I have
read many case histories of depression following the
restoration of sight, and, according to the psychologists, the disorder is related to this superabundance,
this constant stream of simultaneous impressions.

Were my other senses sharper when I was blind? I
am skeptical of Hull when he says that with blindness
the skin of his face and hands became extraordinarily
sensitive to sunlight, and he could tell whether a light
bulb was on in a ceiling simply by turning his face toward it. Bjarnhof touched the hand of the girl he loved
and knew when her eyes darkened. And Lusseyran
claimed that his hands took on a life of their own, becoming more supple, measuring, weighing, pressing,
letting the object touch them as well as touching it.
This is clearly more than the differing warmth between black and white surfaces in sunlight. I can only
think there is something more than blindness going on

in these descriptions of a sixth sense. We are dealing with the occult.

"Trees and rocks came to me and printed their shape upon me like fingers leaving their impression in wax," Lusseyran said. He is a Saint Francis who happens also to be blind.

I can attest, however, that the blind develop a "sense of obstacles," rather like bats, a "gross obstacle vision" or "facial vision." It is the "videation" and "sound-shadows" of Potok. As Lusseyran put it, "Like drugs, blindness heightens certain sensations, giving sudden and often disturbing sharpness to the senses of hearing and touch."

The best explanation I have ever read for this blind acuteness comes from Russell who uses neither cane nor guide dog yet demonstrates an amazing ability in judging direction and distance. He hears the sound of his footsteps bouncing back like an echo. When the echo hits one of his ears before the other, he moves his head until the sounds are equal and thus knows when he faces the object. He knows the time and distance between his own footstep and his ear. Comparing that with the echo from an object, he can judge its distance. Russell's description supports those studies that show the blind perception of objects as fully explainable by sound waves and hearing, yet no study can negate the remarkability of such skill.

I cannot claim to have gone far with that sensibility. I do remember that while swimming I could tell when I was near the edge of the pool, coming to the end of a lap. The sound of the water was as telltale as a tocsin and strong enough to be called facial vision. But that is a talent that on a limited level sighted people enjoy, too, simply by closing their eyes. Wagner agrees with me: "I can't hear any sounds you couldn't hear yourself if you were listening." If there is any resultant sharpening of the senses, it is far more the result of hard work by the blind than any physiological changes.

If there is more extraordinary acuity, however, it comes chiefly to those blinded early in life. I was not young when blinded, and it takes time, as well as a supple mind and an alert body, to develop such awareness. Facial vision is like a foreign language, muscle tone, or the whites of your eyes. Youth helps.

I never perceived enlargements in my experience with blindness. I know that the National Federation of the Blind will vigorously dispute me and claim that I have fallen in with detrimental stereotypes, but I fear I mostly felt the reverse, a perception of diminishment, a symphony without the violins (Lusseyran called it a violin with slackened strings). I passed through many of the emotional stages described by psychologist JoAnn LeMaistre (who suffers from multiple sclerosis)—anger over the slow realization that the medical profession cannot help, depression over "the phantom psyche" ("what might I have done without blindness"), reconstruction and renewal as one begins to accept the inevitable. If I ever felt less than a whole person, it was only a stage. But I do think that through the process there must be character changes. After four years of blindness, Hull thinks he is now shier, unable or unwilling to converse with the stranger in a bar.

I found it so hard to pick up clues to strangers, to fumble with names without faces, that I appreciate Hull's shyness. I think with backgrounds gone, memories of events grew sometimes cloudier. The temptation was always there to turn in on oneself. In my fifteen years I believe I had gradually come to care less about that visible world for the loss of which I initially tried so hard to compensate. The visual aspects of people or the environment came somehow to seem outside of me, beside the point. As Hull put it, "One begins to take up residence in another world." It is the Tiresias sex change in character terms.

To talk about wholeness is to ask for trouble. I realize

that even five senses are not complete when surveying atoms and nebulas; who is to say, then, that four senses are not a full deck? Only the definition changes, the total gestalt, not the basic implication. Blindness should thus be merely a reorganization as a unit, an entire unit, within new limits. Chevigny uses the example of a four-wheeled wagon breaking a wheel, moving the remaining one to the center, and becoming a functioning three-wheeler. The lizard loses his tail but goes on behaving as a whole lizard with new dimensions.

Assuming, then, the possibility of redefining wholeness, let's return to the earlier question of advantages in blindness. Disability is a great teacher, and if one listens, she teaches with conviction about pride and vanity and limitations. I like Beisser's response to the hypothetical question of whether after years of confinement he would like to return to able-bodiedness. He answered with another question, "What would I have to give up?" And this is not the answer of a Pollyanna. It is a not-so-subtle reminder that joy is always balanced by sadness, that the two are forever interlocked.

I have a suspicion that the blind feel greater kinship with the dispossessed. Clark certainly does:

Pickers through garbage cans. Sleepers in doorways. I know them. They are talking to me. Because of my trouble of course; puts me in their camp. On pretty crummy grounds, some would think; they'd say I have no right to claim their society.

External signs of power like Cadillacs and Brooks Brothers suits are not effective with the blind; the powerful, as well as the objects of prejudice, must approach the blind to make their point. But I do not know how far to carry this argument. Blindness did not make me a bleeding-heart liberal, which I was long before I went blind. Yet I know there is something liberating about not seeing an unkempt beard, a stained shirt, the color of skin, and the shapes of noses. Some of the props for prejudice are simply knocked out, and I would like to believe that the result is beneficial. There must be a reason for the portrayal of justice as blind.

I weathered the hard acceptance of dependence and vulnerability. I hope I never courted or cherished them, as some distorted minds secretly do. There were times when I thought the greatest burden was the realization that I could carry very little through without help of other, sighted people. I was bound to my braille watch, to the arrival of readers and drivers, to the unacceptability of taking an extra half hour because if I did someone would be kept waiting. No matter how hard I might try to be free, to write my own books, to deliver my own lectures, to provide for my own family, my daily life was the flip side of individualism. Blindness demands dependence and cooperation, like the buttons on the back of a Shaker shirt, sewn there, deliberately unreachable, to teach the brotherhood of mankind.

Yet looking back, that dependence is only a short step from the dependence of sighted life. Blindness is a dependent world within a dependent world, the weaker symbiotic link that better understands its symbiosis. When I read Beisser's words on this subject, "We are not alone, even if our eyes tell us we are," I wondered if he was implying that without eyes it may be easier to see our interdependence. If so, I can tell him that it is even clearer when sight returns.

As I have said, I found it easy sometimes to identify myself with my disability. I was not a man; I was a blind man. I was not a professor; I was a blind professor. Sacks's Tourette's patient Ray once said, "Suppose you *could* take away the tics. What would be left? I consist of tics—there is nothing else." Sacks concluded that Ray could not imagine life without Tourette's, nor would he care for it. And when the drug Haldol made it possible for him to escape the disability, he regularly went off Haldol to return to his disabled self. Another of Sacks's patients associated her disability with sanity and health. And Dostoevsky is reputed to have claimed that he would not exchange his seizures "for all the joys that life may bring."

That identification with disability, especially when it gave supporting compensations, led inevitably to a certain comfort in maintaining the disability. In my case, however, that comfort was wrested from me by the unexpected surgery. I was not allowed to retain the illusion. And in returning to sight, I was forced to see that health and disability are one. We all live as both winners and losers, sometimes one, sometimes the other: sometimes spry, sometimes disabled; sometimes sighted, sometimes blind. One of my blind friends calls everyone else "temporarily able-bodied."

Anyone who thinks with me for a moment would agree that there are far more tragic circumstances than blindness. The blind can still love, and with all the sight in the world, the absence of love would form a handicap hardly commensurate with an income tax exemption. Some blind lose what LeMaistre calls ableheartedness, and that is indeed a tragedy. Darkness at least has a direction to it, if only seeking light, whereas nothingness bears no compass at all. Both light and dark can be murdered by indifference.

Miracle workers do not deal with indifference, yet one of their favorite tasks is confronting blindness. From Jesus to Potok's bee-woman, blindness is the stuff of miracles. How many people have told me that my second sight is a miracle? If what they mean is a blessing, there can be no doubt. I feel like Helen Keller, who invoked a sense of the miraculous when Anne Sullivan come into her life:

Thus I came up out of Egypt and stood before Sinai, and a power divine touched my spirit and gave it sight, so that I beheld many wonders. And from the sacred mountain I heard a voice which said, "Knowledge is love and light and vision."

What might she have written had she regained her sight!

In "Saint Joan," Shaw says that a miracle is any event that creates faith. I certainly now have more faith in medical science. But for all I know, my second sight may be more than science. The timing seemed beyond the ordinary flow of events: the nurse's call to offer an appointment the following day; the juxtaposition of Dr. Killeen and me; the sudden rise of eye pressure that forced the surgery; the unexpected clarity of the interior of the eye after the years of deterioration. I do not wish to say where science ends and miracles begin.

Call my sight, any sight, what you will, I know and feel utter, overwhelming gratitude that cannot be far removed from a renewed faith in a purpose larger than science itself.

Barring the unforeseen, it seems that the overall pattern of my life will be the initial birth out of womb-blindness into sight, the descent into fifteen years of another blindness, and then the rebirth into sight. There will be one final plunge, I know, one last blindness (or one last sight?). When that comes, I stand fortunate because like Tiresias, I have tasted the two alternatives before.

Unlike Tiresias, I will not advise the gods on sex (notwithstanding my new green socks) and not even on the delights of darkness and light. If they were to question me on blindness and sight, if one like Hera suggested that I renounce my wicked ways of seeing to understand my former sightlessness, I think I would mumble a few words about the two faces of reality. I might revive the old cliché that sighted or blind, we are all disabled. I would beg forgiveness that I had once aspired to become a mini-king in the country of the blind, and I would try to recite a poem I read somewhere about every singing bird concealing within itself "a bat in love with darkness."

Note and Acknowledgments

Since this essay is without footnotes, I have placed an annotated copy with references for quotations in the Rivera Library, University of California, Riverside. It is available through interlibrary loan.

I am most grateful to each of the following people who have read portions of the manuscript and/or offered suggestions: H. G. Jim Burns, John Mack Faragher, Kathy Fischbach, August Frugé, Edwin S. Gaustad, Mary Gazlay, Michelle Hoffnung, Jeanne L. Killeen, M.D., Lou Masur, Werner Marti, Stephen Munz, M.D., James B. Parsons, Roy Harvey Pearce, Oliver Sacks, M.D., Frederic Schroeder, Don Stoutenborough, David Warren, Candace Watt, and Judith Zaragoza. William Brandon should have special thanks for his initial and continuing encouragement. To Stanley Holwitz of the University of California Press, I owe gratitude for his enthusiasm ("Run, don't walk, to the nearest post box"). Working with him and with my editors, Michelle Nordon, Diana Feinberg, and Sheila Berg, has been a rewarding joy.

Every page of the book says thank you to Shirley.

Bibliography

Baird, Joseph L., and Deborah A. Workman, eds. *Toward Solomon's Mountain: The Experience of Disability in Poetry*. Philadelphia: Temple University Press, 1986.

Beisser, Arnold R. *Flying Without Wings: Personal Reflections on Being Disabled*. New York: Doubleday, 1989.

Bjarnhof, Karl. *The Stars Grow Pale*. New York: Knopf, 1958.

———. *The Good Light*. New York: Knopf, 1959.

Blackhall, David Scott. *The Way I See It*. London: John Baker, 1970.

Chevigny, Hector, and Sydell Braverman. *The Adjustment of the Blind*. New Haven: Yale University Press, 1950.

———. *My Eyes Have a Cold Nose*. New Haven: Yale University Press, 1962.

Clark, Eleanor. *Eyes, Etc.: A Memoir*. New York: Pantheon, 1977.

Dubus, Andre. *Broken Vessels*. Boston: David Godine, 1991.

Farrell, Gabriel. *The Story of Blindness*. Cambridge: Harvard University Press, 1956.

French, Richard S. *From Homer to Helen Keller*. New York: American Foundation for the Blind, 1932.

Grindle, Lincoln. *Living with Cataracts: A Layman's Guide to Cataract Surgery*. South Laguna, Calif.: Lasenda, 1982.

Gwaltney, John L. *The Thrice Shy: Cultural Accommodation to Blindness and Other Disasters in a Mexican Community*. New York: Columbia University Press, 1970.

Hocken, Sheila. *Emma and I*. New York: E. P. Dutton, 1977.

Hoffer, Eric. *In Our Time*. New York: Harper and Row, 1976.

———. *Truth Imagined*. New York: Harper and Row, 1983.

Hull, John M. *Touching the Rock: An Experience of Blindness*. London: SPCK, 1990.

Jernigan, Kenneth, ed. *What You Should Know About Blindness, Services for the Blind, and the Organized Blind Movement*. Baltimore: National Federation of the Blind, 1992.

Keller, Helen. *The Story of My Life*. Intro. by Robert Russell. New York: Scholastic, 1967.

Kemper, Robert G. *An Elephant's Ballet: One Man's Successful Struggle with Sudden Blindness*. New York: Seabury, 1977.

Koestler, Frances A. *The Unseen Minority: A Social History of Blindness in the United States*. New York: David McKay, 1976.

Krentz, Harold. *To Race the Wind*. New York: Putnam's, 1972.

LeMaistre, JoAnn. *Beyond Rage: The Emotional Impact of Chronic Physical Illness*. Oak Park, Ill.: Alpine Guild, 1985.

Lusseyran, Jacques. *And There Was Light*. Boston: Little, Brown, 1963.

McCoy, Marie Bell. *Journey Out of Darkness*. New York: David McKay, 1963.

Mackiw-Kraus, Ellen, and G. Richard O'Connor, eds. *Uveitis: Pathophysiology and Therapy*. 2d ed. New York: Thieme Medical Publishers, 1986.

Matson, Floyd. *Walking Alone and Marching Together: A History of the Organized Blind Movement in the United States, 1940–1990*. Baltimore: National Federation of the Blind, 1990.

Mehta, Ved. *Vedi*. New York: Oxford University Press, 1981.

———. *The Stolen Light*. New York: Norton, 1989.

Miller, Jonathan. *The Body in Question*. New York: Random House, 1978.

Murphy, Robert F. *The Body Silent*. New York: Henry Holt, 1987.

Nussenblatt, Robert B., and Alan G. Palestine. *Uveitis: Fundamentals and Clinical Practice*. Chicago: Year Book Medical, 1989.

Packard, Richard B., and Fiona Kinnear. *Manual of Cataract and Intraocular Lens Surgery*. Edinburgh: Churchill Livingstone, 1991.

Perkins, Edward Sylvester. *Uveitis and Toxoplasmosis*. Boston: Little, Brown, 1961.

Potok, Andrew. *Ordinary Daylight: Portrait of an Artist Going Blind*. New York: Holt, Rinehart, and Winston, 1980.

Rivers, Linda. *Through Her Eyes: A True Story of Love, Miracles and Realities*. Hillsboro, Ore.: Beyond Words Publishing, 1990.

Russell, Robert. *To Catch an Angel: Adventures in the World I Cannot See*. New York: Vanguard, 1962.

Sacks, Oliver. *The Man Who Mistook His Wife for a Hat*. New York: Harper and Row, 1987.

———. *Seeing Voices: A Journey into the World of the Deaf*. Berkeley: University of California Press, 1989.

Sanford, Charlotte, and Lester David. *Second Sight: A Miraculous Story of Vision Regained*. New York: M. Evans & Co., 1979.

Schlaegel, T. F., Jr. *Essentials of Uveitis*. Boston: Little, Brown, 1969.

Scott, Robert A. *The Making of Blind Men: A Study of Adult Socialization*. New York: Russell Sage, 1969.

Senden, Marius von. *Space and Sight: The Perception of Space and Shape in the Congenitally Blind Before and After Operation.* Glencoe, Ill.: Free Press, 1960.

Smith, Ronald E., and Robert A. Nozik. *Uveitis: A Clinical Approach to Diagnosis and Management.* 2d ed. Baltimore: Williams and Wilkins, 1989.

Sontag, Susan. *Illness as Metaphor.* New York: McGraw-Hill, 1978.

Sullivan, Tom, and Derek Gill. *If You Could See What I Hear.* New York: Harper and Row, 1975.

Taylor, Judy. *As I See It.* London: Grafton, 1989.

Thurber, James. *My Life and Hard Times.* New York: Harper and Brothers, 1933.

———. *Selected Letters of James Thurber.* Edited by Helen Thurber and Edward Weeks. Boston: Little, Brown, 1980.

———. *Conversations with James Thurber.* Edited by Thomas Fensch. Jackson: University Press of Mississippi, 1989.

Vajda, Albert. *Lend Me an Eye.* New York: St. Martin's, 1975.

Valvo, Alberto. *Sight Restoration after Long-Term Blindness: The Problems and Behavior Patterns of Visual Rehabilitation.* New York: American Foundation for the Blind, 1971.

Wagner, Sally. *How Do You Kiss a Blind Girl?* Springfield, Ill.: C. C. Thomas, 1986.

Wells, Herbert George. "The Country of the Blind." In *Works of H. G. Wells.* 10: 601–636. New York: Charles Scribner's Sons, 1925.

Yates, Elizabeth. *The Lighted Heart.* New York: E. P. Dutton, 1960.

Index

Designer: Cynthia Krupat
Compositor: Wilsted & Taylor
Text: 11/18 Primer
Display: Primer
Printer: Haddon Craftsmen Inc.
Binder: Haddon Craftsmen Inc.